“All Possible Art”

“All Possible Art”

George Herbert’s *The Country Parson*

Kristine A. Wolberg

Fairleigh Dickinson

Madison • Teaneck
Fairleigh Dickinson University Press

Associated University Presses
2010 Eastpark Boulevard
Cranbury, NJ 08512

The paper used in this publication meets the requirements of the American National Standard for Permanence of Paper for Printed Library Materials Z39.48–1984.

Library of Congress Cataloging-in-Publication Data

Wolberg, Kristine A., 1956-
"All possible art" : George Herbert's The country parson / Kristine A. Wolberg.
p. cm.
Includes bibliographical references and index.
ISBN 978-0-8386-4170-5 (alk. paper)
1. Herbert, George, 1593-1633—Criticism and interpretation. 2. Herbert, George, 1593-1633. Priest to the temple. 3. Christian poetry, English—Early modern, 1500-1700. 4. Pastoral theology—Early works to 1800. 5. Spiritual life in literature. 6. Theology in literature. I. Title.

PR3508.W65 2008
821'.3—dc22

2008003079

PRINTED IN THE UNITED STATES OF AMERICA

To Dale

Contents

Acknowledgments

"I Struck the board, and cry'd No more."

PROFESSOR BEATRICE BATSON'S DRAMATIC READING OF "THE COLLAR" from the Bemerton pulpit inspired my interest in Herbert studies. Walter Davis, in his excellent discussions of the metaphysical poets, initiated the journey of which this book is the end. My graduate adviser, Carol Stillman, originally suggested considering *The Country Parson* in the light of the courtesy tradition. She proved a companionable guide and mentor through the early stages of research and writing. Thomas Werge helped me further along with his understanding of the period as well as his generosity with time and expert editing. Sidney Gottlieb's kindness and practical advice encouraged me toward publication. My husband, Dale Wolberg, has walked furthest along this road with me. Without his support and help, none of this would have been possible. My heartfelt thanks go to each of these.

Thanks too go to the editors of the *John Donne Journal* and the *George Herbert Journal* for their permission to reprint material here that originally appeared in slightly different forms on their pages.

“All Possible Art”

Introduction

George Herbert's prose work, *The Priest to the Temple* or, as Herbert entitled it, *The Country Parson*, is the only work George Herbert prepared for publication. Despite Herbert's commitment to the piece, over the years it has received only a limited amount of attention for its own sake, especially when compared to the extensive criticism and commentaries devoted to his poetical work, *The Temple*. Historically, critics have shown interest in *The Country Parson* largely in the service of biography or readings of Herbert's poetry.[1] The works of criticism dedicated to *The Country Parson* tend to be largely historical, political, or sociological in nature and their primary focus is on the piece as historical artifact, shedding light on Herbert or his times.[2]

Perhaps one reason for the lack of interest in *The Country Parson* as literature is a general unfamiliarity with the genre of the clerical manual. To a reader familiar with the period's other "advice to clergy," *The Country Parson* excites curiosity. There is far more here than ecclesiastical prose and sectarian party politics. *The Country Parson* is indeed so outstanding among other works of its type to suggest that Herbert was artfully shaping the genre to some purpose. This contention, in fact, is one of the important conclusions of this study. Through exploring Herbert's theme, form, topics, emphasis, context, and possible models, we shall find that *The Country Parson* is a carefully conceived and executed work, making sophisticated use of popular sacred and secular materials for a calculated effect, and certainly worth attention in its own right as part of Herbert's literary legacy.

In an effort to initiate discussion on *The Country Parson*, chapter 1 of this study proceeds somewhat polemically. Here Herbert's treatment of his central theme, the doctrine and life of a model priest, is shown to be anything but pedestrian or predictable. His unexpected focus on the life of the country parson—as opposed to the parson's beliefs and doctrinal purity—issues further into three surprising emphases. Herbert stresses the importance of appearances while minimizing the role of the parson's inner life; he exalts the efficacy of experience rather than that of doctrine; and "good works" seem to usurp the central role usually assigned to faith in Protestant thinking. *The Country Parson* should evoke interest based on its independent treatment of these theological issues alone. When compared with other manuals, Herbert's becomes even more intriguing.

Chapter 2 studies *The Country Parson* in the context of other contemporary clerical literature. It demonstrates that, while on some points Herbert seems to be directly opposing certain trends in the largely Puritan genre, his overall strategy is to provide a balanced *via media* between what he calls the "superstition" of the high church and the "slovenliness" of the low. In areas of doctrine, exegesis, homiletics, and church appearances, Herbert recommends strategies that cross party lines; he brings elements from the Puritan and Anglo-Catholic traditions together in his ideal pastor.

Since *The Country Parson* is so unique among clerical manuals, it seems clear that Herbert was deliberately shaping it in a purposeful, even artful, way. Chapter 3 submits that Herbert wrote *The Country Parson* after the manner of the popular Renaissance courtesy book. In purpose, temper, diction, subject matter, and classical influence, *The Country Parson* shows undeniable affinities to the courtesy genre. Viewing *The Country Parson* in light of the courtesy tradition helps explain some of its unusual emphases. The second half of chapter 3 focuses on the "problem" uncovered in chapter 1: of Herbert's showing a decided preference for experience over doctrine, "book learning," and other forms of formal instruction. This preference turns out to be consistent with contemporary aristocratic values and very much a part of traditional courtesy instruction.

Chapter 4 continues the discussion of chapter 3 by suggesting a specific work upon which Herbert may have modeled *The Country Parson*. Stefano Guazzo's *The Civile Conversation*, an Italian courtesy book quite well known to Elizabethan Englishmen, was particularly well suited for the task. Pious, scriptural, and proverb laden, *The Civile Conversation* would have strongly appealed to Herbert's tastes. Further, Guazzo's reluctant criticism of the clergy could have provided Herbert with the inspiration for a courtesy book written specifically to ministers. Guazzo complains of the clergy that, while their doctrine may be impeccable, their less than exemplary lives are not to be imitated. Aware of identical criticism made of his own colleagues, Herbert devotes *The Country Parson* to perfecting the lives—and showing comparatively little interest in the doctrine or beliefs—of the English clergy. Other available manuals focus on the heart, beliefs, and inner life of the parson and his people; Herbert's thrust is decidedly outward. Responding to a need for a handbook on behavior and manners, Herbert writes his manual in the form of the genre specifically dedicated to outer appearances: the courtesy book.

The relationship between Herbert's treatment of appearances and that of the Italian "fathers of courtesy" is the subject of chapter 5. Here it becomes evident that while Herbert's techniques for artful self-fashioning might have been borrowed from the pages of Castiglione or Della Casa, Herbert's purposes could not. On this point, we find a remarkable similarity between *The Country Parson* and Guazzo's *The Civile Conversation*. Herbert and Guazzo exhibit a striking unity of purpose regarding appearances in a way that makes them both anomalous among writers in their genres.

In following the techniques and strategies of Guazzo and other courtesy authors, *The Country Parson* exhibits the same "complexity dormant within apparent simplicity" which Herbert's poetry is said to employ.[3] When this "complexity" was finally recognized, *The Temple* was delivered from obscurity. Perhaps it is time for *The Country Parson* to be similarly delivered, and admired, indeed, even celebrated.

That George Herbert was familiar with the forms and strategies of the courtesy book has long been put forward. As early as 1949, M. M. Mahood wrote that *The Country Parson,* "has the form and tone and, to a certain extent, the temper of Caroline courtesy-books."[4] Marion White Singleton interpreted the poems of *The*

Temple as the word of a courtier exposing the deeply corrupt, unactualizable pattern of courtliness, while trying to "recover . . . whatever ideal *potentia* it still might possess."[5] Michael Schoenfeldt's *Prayer and Power: George Herbert and Renaissance Courtship* notes that both "The Church-porch" and the world of *The Country Parson* are "preoccupied by the rhetorical aspects of proper behavior," and he develops at length his thesis that "The Temple is itself a kind of spiritualized courtesy book."[6] Ronald Cooley has observed that *The Country Parson* "seeks to address the deficiencies of both the old and the new clergy, using the method of criticism and exhortation through hyperbolic flattery that was a standard device of courtly literature."[7] Cristina Malcolmson's biography of Herbert describes his early aristocratic influences and courtly coterie and identifies the speaker of many of Herbert's poems as "an upper-class man trained at the University and in the rituals of courtesy."[8]

Despite near universal agreement that Herbert knew and used the methods of courtesy and despite the many references made to courtesy literature in the criticism of Herbert's poetry, no extensive study links Herbert's interest in courtesy themes and techniques with *The Country Parson*. This investigation hopes to show that *The Country Parson* is a carefully crafted piece of literary prose, inspired significantly by the Renaissance courtesy tradition. As the courtesy book author sought to model proper behavior and manners for the courtly gentleman, in *The Country Parson,* Herbert used "all possible art"[9] to set down the "Form and Character of a true Pastour," that he and his fellow clergy may have a "Mark to aim at" (224).

1
Doctrine and Life in *The Country Parson*

Lord, how can man preach thy eternall word?
    He is a brittle crazie glasse:
Yet in thy temple thou dost him afford
    This glorious and transcendent place,
    To be a window, through thy grace.

But when thou dost anneal in glasse thy storie,
    Making thy life to shine within
The holy Preachers; then the light and glorie
    More rev'rend grows, & more doth win:
    Which else shows watrish, bleak, & thin.

Doctrine and life, colours and light, in one
    When they combine and mingle, bring
A strong regard and aw: but speech alone
    Doth vanish like a flaring thing,
    And in the eare, not conscience ring.
                —George Herbert, "The Windows"

COMING FROM A POET AND PREACHER, GEORGE HERBERT'S "THE Windows" is surprising. It expresses a decided lack of confidence in language. Alone, speech is a vanishing, flaring thing, which may ring in the listener's ear, but cannot communicate on a significant level. Helen Vendler describes "The Windows" as "notable in being one of the few poems in *The Temple* having an 'unhappy ending.'"[1] It is "unhappy" because it contends that, without an appropriate way of life to support them, words are impotent. Vendler points out that Herbert's insistent intertwining of life and art makes some critics uncomfortable. Statements like, "If I please [God], I write fine and wittie" ("The Forerunners") reflect "a poetic that might not succeed for a poet of lesser genius."[2]

But "The Windows" is not about the intertwining of life and art as much as it is about the intertwining of life and doctrine. And this may make at least some critics equally uncomfortable. "The Windows" is a poem not about language in general but about religious language. It begins with this question: "Lord, how can man preach thy eternall word?" Herbert answers himself emblematically: The preacher is a "brittle crazie glass" in which Christ "anneals" His "storie." The colors of the stained glass represent Christ's doctrine, which appears "watrish, bleak, and thin," without the light of Christ's life shining through the preacher's life. When a preacher's doctrine and life reflect Christ's, however, he commands a "strong regard and aw."

That the ideal preacher practices what he preaches is an uninteresting commonplace. What is very interesting about this poem is what Herbert says about doctrine, or rather, what Herbert does not say. What he does not say is that doctrine is efficacious no matter who preaches it. If there is indeed anything about the ending of the poem that is "unhappy," it is that doctrine alone is "watrish, bleak, and thin," and powerless to change lives. While thus undercutting the power of doctrine, Herbert underscores the power of right living. The second stanza of "The Windows" is entirely devoted to Christ's life shining through the life of the good preacher. The third stanza expresses the uselessness of speech alone. Clearly, "life" takes over in this poem, leaving doctrine in some secondary and undefined place.

If "The Windows" were all we had of Herbert's thoughts on doctrine and life, we might dismiss its unorthodox bent as a momentary theological speculation. But the theme of "The Windows" is developed in length in Herbert's prose work*, A Priest to the Temple* or*, The Country Parson*. It is, in fact, the central concern of the book. In the first chapter of *The Country Parson* Herbert makes clear his theme, the life and doctrine of the good priest: "a Priest is to do that which Christ did, and after his manner, both for Doctrine and Life" (225:18–19). Herbert's idea of doing that which Christ did regarding doctrine and life is somewhat peculiar for a Protestant of Herbert's day. What following Christ in these areas meant for Herbert was placing a definite priority on right living and less importance on doctrinal issues. *The Country Parson*'s focus is squarely on the good life, on practical Christian living rather than on theological correctness or doctrinal purity.[3]

The overall structure of *The Country Parson* reveals this emphasis. After five introductory chapters—defining his subject (chapter 1), audience (chapter 2), and theme: Life (chapter 3) and Doctrine (chapters 4 and 5)—Herbert devotes the first two-thirds of his book (chapters 6 through 29) primarily to the practical side of the parson's life: the parson praying, preaching, on Sundays, comforting, in journey, catechizing, punishing, and so on. Only as he nears the end of his treatise does Herbert begin to become more doctrinal in his focus. Chapters 30 through 37 are essentially theological, dealing with such subjects as providence, Christian liberty, and holiness.

Herbert's strategy is unlike that of other comparable authors. The typical Protestant writer of Herbert's day created a theological manual after the Reformation paradigm of salvation, dealing with sanctification only after justification.[4] That is, he discussed how to be a better Christian only after he explained how to be a Christian. The first order of business was always belief, not behavior, because true sanctification could only occur in a regenerate soul. There was no use talking about living a better life to someone who was "spiritually dead." This rule of treating doctrine before life or belief before behavior was followed in manuals for clergy as well as laymen.

Richard Baxter, for example, in *The Reformed Pastor,* devoted considerable space to doctrine before touching on practical ethics. *The Reformed Pastor* begins with a long introductory chapter urging pastors to be certain of their own belief. He laments that "so many men become preachers before they are Christians."[5] It is only after extended discussions on the need for genuine belief in the true doctrine that Baxter can begin to discuss holy living and the duties of a parson. William Ames's *The Marrow of Sacred Divinity* graphically demonstrates the habit of treating doctrine before life. He divides his treatise into two parts, part 1 dealing exclusively with doctrine ("faith") and part 2 with life ("observance"). Ames introduces the structure of his discourse this way: "It is characteristic of this division . . . that it follows from the nature of the object. Since the beginning or first act of the spiritual life, which is the proper concern of theology, is faith and the second act or operation of that principle is observance, it follows that . . . faith holds the first place and spiritual observance the second, for no vital actions or life are forthcoming except where there is an inborn principle of life."[6] As Ames states here, it seems only natural that one should treat theory before practice, doctrine before life.

In *The Country Parson* Herbert not only reverses this usual order, but he deemphasizes doctrine here as he does in "The Windows." Again and again in *The Country Parson* life overshadows doctrine. The roles normally given to doctrine are usurped by life, as when life takes over didactic functions normally assigned to doctrine, and public life replaces the usually central place given to doctrine internalized or personal belief. Each of these choices is significant.

In *The Country Parson* life experience proves a better teacher than doctrine. Herbert provides in his second chapter some advice to his readers still in the university. To those preparing for the ministry he cautions that a sound doctrinal training alone does not make a good minister: "Some in a preparatory way, whose aim and labour must be not only to get knowledg, but to subdue and mortifie all lusts and affections: and not to think, that when they have read the Fathers, or Schoolmen, a Minister is made, and the thing done" (226:10–12). Taken by itself, this admonition to seminary students to "subdue and mortifie all lusts and affections" seems eminently sensible and traditional. But Herbert's treatment of this theme is curious. Here he seems to pass an unusually harsh judgment upon one of the favorite pastimes of scholars, theoretical discussion: "Curiosity in prying into speculative and unprofitable questions, is [a] great stumbling block to the holinesse of Scholars. These and many other spirituall wickednesses in high places doth the Parson fear" (238:18–21). Herbert contrasts speculative discussion, a "spirituall wickedness," with holiness. Quibbling over minute points of doctrine must not distract one from the more important task of sanctification. What doctrinal issues Herbert here considers "speculative" and "unprofitable" is not clear. What is certain is Herbert's preference for having scholars look to their lives rather than to at least some doctrinal issues.

Herbert continues with this train of thought, suggesting that when scholars leave the seminary, life experience will prove more useful than theory. In advising the seminarians, he suggests that they set down their books and look around them: "Country people are full of . . . petty injustices, being cunning to make use of another, and spare themselves; And Scholars ought to be diligent in the observation of these, and driving of their generall Schoole rules even to the smallest actions of Life; which while they dwell in their bookes they will never find; but . . . doing their duty faithfully, they will soon discover" (265:33–266:4). The relevancy of "school rules" to life simply cannot be known on the theoretical level. Life experience must unlock the power of doctrine, for otherwise scholars will "never find" the usefulness of it.

Herbert does not only suggest that life must complement doctrine, but he believes that in some situations life experience is more important than doctrine. For instance, when describing how to prepare a teaching, Herbert does not provide lists of doctrinal treatises, commentaries, or other typical homiletic aids. Instead, he suggests that the parson look to his life. The parson's own experience in spiritual victories will provide him better material than all "rules of temperance out of bookes" (278:21). An existential apprehension of virtue is of far more value in teaching than naked doctrine. Sermons should proceed from the experience of virtue rather than mere intellectual understanding: "So that the Parson having studied, and mastered all his lusts and affections within, and the whole Army of Temptations without, hath ever so many sermons penn'd as he hath victories" (278:21–24). Here Herbert uses language usually associated with written expressions of doctrine to describe experience. We read "the Parson having studied" and expect the object of the phrase to be the title of a doctrinal treatise. Instead Herbert tells us that sermons are produced from studying life. A good life, Herbert maintains, makes for the best sort of teaching. His examples further imply a decided preference for experience over dogma: "Hee that hath considered how to carry himself at table about his appetite, if he tell this to another, preacheth; and *much more feelingly, and judiciously*, then he writes his rules of temperance out of bookes . . . He that hath been sick of a Consumption, and knows what recovered him, is a Physitian so far as he meetes with the same disease, and temper; and *can much better, and particularly do it,* then he that is generally learned, and was never sick" (278:18–29, my italics).

Better than "rules . . . out of bookes," better than being "generally learned" is personal experience for teaching others. Herbert takes this thinking one step further. A "holy life," Herbert writes, "even itself is a Sermon" (278:14). The triumph of life here is complete. Not only does life take over doctrine's role as the source for the sermon, it becomes the sermon itself.

This emphasis on experience is not incidental or unconscious. Herbert clearly draws attention to it in chapter 33, "The Parson's Library." All of Herbert's preceding chapters have plainly declared their contents in their titles, e.g., "The Parson's Church" is simply about the church building and its accoutrements and "The Parson in his house" discusses household business and domestic relations. But here Herbert creates an expectation in order to disappoint it and make his point. After reading the title, "The Parson's Library," we anticipate a discussion of books and authors. Those who know Herbert as the Cambridge orator and master poet may have especially high expectations in looking for those works which helped form his thinking. But instead we find: "The Countrey Parson's Library is a holy Life" (278:11). If Herbert were ever going to endorse theological writers or doctrinal treatises, this would be the place. But just where we most expect it, in a discussion about the Parson's personal library, he refuses to do so. Instead, he surprises expectations to make a point important to him: for teaching others, a holy life is more important than a library full of sound doctrine.

Herbert has still more striking claims to make on the behalf of life experience. We have seen that for teaching he recommends holiness in life more than he does doctrine in books. In "The Parson arguing," Herbert further suggests that good behavior is a better apologetic than good arguments. Once again life takes precedence over doctrine. In Herbert's three-part strategy for converting those who "hold strange Doctrins" (262:20), the clear emphasis is on holy living rather than holy thinking. Note the order of his agenda: "The first means he useth is Prayer . . . The second means is a very loving, and sweet usage of them . . . The third means is the observation what is the main foundation, and pillar of their cause" (262:21–29). Only after one has tried the "arguments" of holy living should the parson begin a doctrinal discourse.

In a chapter like "The Parson arguing" where Herbert is dealing with doctrinal disputes, we expect him to be particularly theoretical, delineating various proofs and arguments for orthodox faith. Again, Herbert defies our expectations. His arguments against "Papist" and "Schismatick" alike are tantalizingly brief —one condensed sentence each. He seems eager to finish with such theorizing and comforts the possibly disappointed reader with the assurance that a holy life will convince where doctrine does not: "having ever besides two great helps and powerful perswaders on his side; the one, a strict religious life; the other an humble and ingenious search of truth . . . which are two great lights able to dazle the eyes of the mis-led" (263:15–19).

The good parson's holy life not only "dazzles" the misled, it also argues for the truth of his doctrine. The above quotation continues, "while they consider, that God cannot be wanting to them in Doctrine, to whom he is so gracious in Life" (263:19–21). Herbert's confidence in the power of holy living seems unbounded. Here holy living establishes the truth of the parson's doctrine. This is a surprising claim. Now it is not uncommon to hear that a good life confirms the authenticity of one's faith (as in James 2:17, "Faith without works is dead.") But the claim that a good life confirms the truth of one's doctrine is unusual, especially for one in the Reformation tradition where revealed doctrine from the Scriptures is truth itself. One problem inherent in Herbert's claim is its suggestion that the truth of Christianity is somehow dependent upon the believer's behavior. Using such an axiom, a nonbeliever could reason, "This Christian lives a gracious life; therefore, his doctrine (Christianity) must be true." But the nonbeliever could just as legitimately reason, "That Christian does not live a gracious life; therefore, Christianity is not true." No traditional understanding of Christianity would tolerate such a relativistic or existential test. The view held by Herbert's contemporaries was: Christianity is true, despite the behavior of individual Christians, not because of it.

To state that "God cannot be wanting to them in Doctrine, to whom he is so gracious in Life" places a remarkable emphasis on the outward behavior of believers. Even if this statement of Herbert's were made off-handedly and not as an apologetic principle, it reveals Herbert's unusual view of doctrine and life. The logical outgrowth of such thinking would be that anyone leading what appeared to be a "strict religious life" (263:16) held to true doctrine. But the New Testament exposed the Pharisees and Sadducees as just such outwardly correct but inwardly impoverished people. Christ condemned them because, while they obeyed the Law in all its outward manifestations, their hearts were far from God: "Woe unto you, scribes and Pharisees, hypocrites! For ye make clean the outside of the cup and of the platter, but within they are full of extortion and excess" (Matthew 23:25).[7] If all those who act correctly also think and believe correctly, Christ never would have said to the religious leaders of his day, "Even so ye also outwardly appear righteous unto men, but within ye are full of hypocrisy and iniquity" (Matthew 23: 28).

In light of such New Testament passages, it is curious that Herbert gives so much attention to the life or behavior of the parson and so little to his heart, thoughts, or beliefs. The kind of attention he gives to the parson's life provides a further curiosity. Where other clerical manuals emphasize the importance of the inner man, his purity of heart and doctrine, Herbert's focus is on the outer man, his appearance and public life.

In *The Country Parson* public life replaces the usually central role given to private belief. Most pastoral letters and manuals make inner qualities such as purity of doctrine, faith, and sincerity their basis for describing the good parson. St. Paul's first letter to Timothy probably provided a model. After the opening greeting, Paul began encouraging the young pastor regarding those most important aspects of the ministry–doctrine, love, a pure heart, and a good conscience: "As I urged you when I was going to Macedonia, remain at Ephesus that you may charge certain persons not to teach any different doctrine . . . the aim of our charge is love that issues from a pure heart and a good conscience and sincere faith" (I Timothy 1:3–5 *Revised Standard Version*).

Commenting on this passage, Calvin answered those who imagine Paul to prefer love ("a good life") to faith ("doctrine") in a pastor: "But here arises a doubt, that Paul appears to prefer 'love' to 'faith.' I reply, they who are of that opinion reason in an excessively childish manner; for, if love is first mentioned, it does not therefore hold the first rank of honour, since Paul shews also that it springs from faith. Now the cause undoubtedly goes before its effect . . . Thus we must begin with faith, and not with love."[8] James Gardiner began his *Advice to Clergy* explaining that the thing most needful for the work of the ministry is "simplicity and sincerity of heart."[9] In his *Reformed Pastor* Richard Baxter gives as his first exhortation to the clergy: "See that the work of saving grace be thoroughly wrought in your own souls."[10] Like William Ames, most Protestant clergy would agree that "faith holds the first place and spiritual observance the second"; that is, pastors should be characterized first by the work of doctrine in their hearts, then by their good works.

But when Herbert describes the perfect clergyman, he reverses this pattern. We know that *The Country Parson* is in fact Herbert's description of the model priest because of his preface to the reader in which he explains: "I have resolved to set down the Form and Character of a true Pastour, that I may have a Mark to aim at: which also I will set as high as I can, since hee shoots higher that threatens the Moon, then hee that aims at a Tree" (224:6). But surprisingly Herbert does not begin his characterization with a treatment of the pastor's state of soul; he begins instead with the externals of life. The parson's public image and observable behavior are Herbert's primary concerns.[11] His description begins: "The Country Parson is exceeding exact in his Life being holy, just, prudent, temperate, bold, grave," not particularly in his heart or character, but in "his wayes" (227:1–3). He explains that the parson must master patience and mortification, not because of what these sins might do to his own spiritual condition, but because these are "the two highest points of Life, wherein a Christian is *most seen*" (227:3–4, my italics). He goes on to warn against "Luxury" because it is a "very visible sin" (227:22). Statements like, "Yet in these points he labours most in those things which are most apt to scandalize his Parish" (227:10–11), reflect Herbert's special attention to the visible side of the ministry. Herbert ends this introductory description with a metaphor, which is telling in its fastidious fixation on externals: "The parson's yea is yea, and nay nay; and his apparell plaine, but reverend, and clean, without spots or dust, or smell; the purity of his mind breaking out and dilating it selfe even to his body, cloaths, and habitation" (228:9–12).

Clearly, Herbert is anxious to advise his readers regarding public appearances. While he mentions "purity of mind," Herbert places an unusual emphasis on outer details of body, clothes and habitation.

If Herbert's interest in externals is unusual, even more surprising are his suggestions to exploit and manipulate them. For example in chapter 6, "The Parson praying," Herbert explains how the appearance of devotion can be used to appropriately affect one's parishioners: "hee may affect also his people, knowing that no Sermon moves them so much to a reverence, which they forget againe, when they come to pray, as a *devout behaviour* in the very act of praying" (231:13–16, my italics). Since this is so, Herbert carefully instructs his readers on how best to *sound* devout: "Accordingly his voyce is humble, his words treatable, and slow; yet not so slow neither, as to let the fervency of the of the supplicant hang and dy between speaking, but with a grave livelinesse, between fear and zeal, pausing yet pressing, he *performes* his duty" (231:16–20, my emphasis). Herbert's choice of "perform" in this context is illuminating. Like an actor, the pastor pays meticulous attention to the sound of his voice. His congregation is his audience. Herbert self-consciously manipulates his prayers. Here his interest is the performance of prayer, not its content, not the pastor's own heartfelt devotion. Other chapters continue this focus on performance and projecting a "holy" appearance.

While chapter 7 often addresses the nature of sermons, the real subject of "The Parson preaching" is the parson. The first eighty-six lines tell the parson how to deliver the sermon, discussing his voice, gestures, facial expressions, and carriage. Only three sentences are actually devoted to expostulation of the biblical text. Unlike nearly all Protestants on the topic of preaching, Herbert chooses to emphasize delivery and not exegesis, the parson's presence, not his text. Here, for example, Herbert describes how the parson is to keep the attention of his audience: "When he preacheth, he procures attention *by all possible art,* both by earnestnesse of speech, it being naturall to men to thinke, that where is much earnestness, there is somewhat worth hearing; and by a diligent, and busy cast of his eye on his auditors, with letting them know, that he observes who marks, and who not (232:30–234:2, my emphasis). There is something of the actor's language here. Herbert recommends "all possible art," bravado, appearances to make men think that there is something worth the hearing. Rather than letting the scripture have its own effect, Herbert recommends "truly affecting, and cordially expressing all that we say" (233:30–31). He even provides lines for the would-be actor/pastor who reads his work: "turning often, and making many Apostrophes to God, as, Oh Lord blesse my people, and teach them this point; or, Oh my Master, on whose errand I come, let me hold my peace, and doe thou speak thy selfe; for thou art Love, and when thou teachest, all art Scholers" (233:32–37). "Some such irradiations scatteringly in the Sermon," Herbert assures his readers, "carry great holiness in them" (233:37–234:1). The appearance of holiness is the goal to which all this acting tends.

Herbert further suggests that the preacher should express "wishes of the peoples good" (234:6–7) in his sermon, for "There is no greater *sign of holinesse,* then procuring, and rejoycing in anothers good" (234:9–10, my emphasis). It is the sign or appearance of holiness rather than holiness itself that Herbert specifically addresses here.

Besides these means, Herbert recommends weaving emotions, even tears, into the sermon at appropriate moments. To defend this practice he cites Jesus's example: "never was there such care of a flock expressed, save in the great shepherd of the fold, who first shed teares over Jerusalem, and afterwards blood. Therefore this care may be learn'd there, and then woven into Sermons" (234:20–23). Herbert makes the purpose of displaying such emotion in the sermons quite clear; it will "*make them ap-*

pear exceeding reverend, and holy" (234:24, my italics). Finally, Herbert suggests that the parson invoke the presence and majesty of God as he preaches. Again, he suggests lines for his readers to recite after which he concludes, "Such discourses *shew* very Holy" (234:35–36, my emphasis).

In "The Parson preaching" we would expect to find expressed commitments to such Protestant doctrines as the centrality of scripture and the primacy of the sermon. Instead, we find Herbert almost entirely absorbed with the preacher himself. And rather than the heart, beliefs, or doctrine of the parson, Herbert describes and seeks to improve the outer form.[12] In his "Note to the Reader" Herbert prepares the reader for just such a focus when he explains, "I have resolved to set down the Form and Character of a true Pastour" (224). We now see clearly what he meant by "Form": the outer appearances and public image. But what does Herbert mean by "Character"? He all but ignores the moral and private dimensions of that word. By "Character," Herbert refers, not to personal integrity, but perhaps to the very popular character sketch genre of his time. Herbert ambiguously uses the second "character" in the following passage to refer either to the sermon or the parson himself: "By these and other means the Parson procures attention; but the character of his Sermon is Holiness; *he* is not witty, or learned, or eloquent, but Holy. *A Character* that Hermogenes never dreamed of" (233:22–25, my italics). "Character" here could refer only to the rhetorical characters of Hermogenes, but Herbert is more likely playing with his words, referring also to the popular character sketch. In fact, Herbert may be suggesting that the parson himself is an artifact, a character sketch figure, a public image consciously crafted for the benefit of his congregation, a character "Hermogenes never dreamed of."[13]

In *The Country Parson* then we find an unabashed concern with fashioning the parson as a public character. Joseph Summers suggests that the modern reader is "shocked" by this attention to appearances because, unlike Herbert, we divorce appearance from reality: "Herbert recommended devices for gaining the appearance of holiness on the assumption that appearance should correspond with reality."[14] All admirers of Herbert are inclined to believe that in George Herbert there was a true holiness corresponding to his public display. But Summers may be too quick to suggest that Herbert's surprising focus is really a problem in the modern reader's mind. Other clergy of Herbert's day were not so eager to cultivate a pious public image, nor did they recommend using "all possible art" to do so. Bishop Gilbert Burnet, in his *Pastoral Care*, for example, specifically forbade such techniques to improve the pastor's presence: "In his sermons he ought, above all things, to study to edify, but not to . . . use vain arts to raise esteem or admiration from [his hearers.]"[15] Perhaps other pastors rejected Herbert's methods because deliberately fashioning a holy appearance seems prohibited by such New Testament teachings as found in Matthew 6:1: "Beware of practicing your piety before men."[16] We must seek another explanation for Herbert's fashioning the parson so as to make him "appear exceeding reverend and holy" (234:24). But first we must observe the breadth of this tendency in *The Country Parson*. Herbert is concerned not only with the appearance of the parson himself, but with the outer form of almost everything related to the parson.

When Herbert describes the way in which a parson should treat his wife, for example, he writes as if his real concern were with how he is perceived to treat her; that is, he wants to appear "just" in all his dealings. Treating his wife with respect will enhance that appearance:

"As hee is just in all things, so is he to his wife also, counting nothing so much his owne, as that he may be unjust unto it. Therefore he gives her respect both *afore her servants, and others*" (238:36–37 my emphasis). Herbert does not direct his readers always to treat their wives with respect, but to behave respectfully before others.

Herbert is concerned with the way his entire household appears in the community and so provides this description: "And when they go abroad, his wife among her neighbours is the beginner of good discourses, his children among children, his servants among other servants; so that as in the house of those that are skill'd in Musick, all are Musicians; so in the house of a Preacher, all are preachers" (240:27–31).

Herbert's focus on the observable behavior of his household is explained in the first line of chapter 10: "The Parson is very exact in the governing of his house, making it a copy and modell for his Parish" (239:6–7). The emphasis of Herbert's writing is not on the beliefs or hearts, in this instance the hearts of his household, but on the public impression made by the parson and those connected with him. Even his furniture and food are chosen for the appearances they make:

"The furniture of his house is very plain, but clean, whole and sweet as his garden can make . . . His fare is plain, and common, but wholesome, what hee hath, is little, but very good . . . lest he goe into the world, esteeming it absurd, that he should exceed, who teacheth others temperance" (241:11–21).

Furthermore, in chapter 13, "The Parson's Church" we find a surprisingly detailed description of the physical condition of the parson's church building:

> The Country Parson hath a speciall care of his Church, that all there be decent, and befitting his Name by which it is called. Therefore first he takes order, that all things be in good repair; as the walls plaistered, windows glazed, floore paved, seats whole, firm, and uniform, especially that the Pulpit, and Desk, and Communion Table, and Font be as they ought, for those great duties that are performed in them. Secondly, that the Church be swept, and kept cleane without dust, or Cobwebs, and at great festivalls strawed, and stuck with boughs, and perfumed with incense. Thirdly, that there be fit, and proper texts of Scripture every where painted, and that all painting be grave, and reverend, not with light colours, or foolish anticks. Fourthly, That all the books appointed by Authority be there, and those not torne, or fouled, but whole and clean, and well bound; and that there be a fitting, and sightly Communion Cloth of fine linnen, with an handsome, and seemly Carpet of good and costly Stuffe, or Cloth, and all kept sweet and clean, in a strong and decent chest, with a Chalice, and Cover, and a Stoop, or Flagon; and a Bason for Almes and offerings; besides which, he hath a Poor-mans Box conveniently seated, to receive the charity of well minded people, and to lay up treasure for the sick and needy. (246:1–22)

The length of this passage alone testifies to the concern Herbert felt for the appearance of his church. His descriptions suggest that the church should appeal to men's senses: "plaistered," "glazed," "paved," "firm," "uniform," "strawed," "stuck with boughs," "perfumed," "painted," "whole and clean," "fine," "handsome and seemly." Herbert's defense of this appeal includes the claim that such attention to appearances can be a testimony to the truth of one's doctrine. Such concern for "externall and indifferent things . . . put[s] them to great shame, who deny the Scripture to be perfect" (246:33–247:2). Once again, as in Herbert's earlier claim that "God cannot be wanting to them in Doctrine, to whom he is so gracious in Life" (263:20–21), Herbert shows his confidence in the ability of external appearances of life to testify to the truth of doctrine.

Herbert's emphasis on observable life is not limited to the parson, his family, or church. We see the same principle applied to his congregation. When dealing with the laity, Herbert seems most interested in things of a decidedly external nature. In chapter 17, "The Parson in Journey," for example, Herbert advises that upon visiting the house of another, the country parson "considers diligently the state thereof Godward" (251:17–18). By this Herbert means that the parson discovers "first, what disorders there are either in Apparell, or Diet, or too open a Buttery" (251:18–20). Only after taking stock of the family habits does Herbert look into their hearts: "Secondly, what means of Piety, whether daily prayers be used, grace, reading of Scriptures" (251:22–23).[17] To the contrary, when other Protestant pastors examine the state of their parishioners "Godward," they seem to be first interested in matters of doctrine and belief. Luther, for example, hotly insisted that pastors who focus on keeping the Old Testament Law and other forms of good works "are not theologians but prattlers." He wrote that the beliefs of the congregation must be the primary interest of pastors: "To neglect faith and yet to teach—what could that accomplish except something of this sort: it has the appearance of piety, but is empty talk?"[18] *The Country Parson* might seem to be cultivating just such an "appearance of piety." Calvin too in his commentaries on the Pastoral Epistles insisted that the pastor's first concern with his flock must be with their beliefs and not their behavior: "Yet he is not so careful about good works as to despise the root—that is, faith—while he is gathering the fruits. He takes account of both parts, and as is highly proper, *assigns the first rank to faith* for he enjoins those "who believed in God" to be zealous of "good works;" by which he means that *faith must go before* in such a manner that good works may follow.[19]

Most of Herbert's Protestant contemporaries agreed with Luther and Calvin. Richard Baxter, for example, displays the more typical pastoral concern with the spiritual state of his charges: "The work of conversion is the great thing we must drive at; after this we must labor with all our might . . . Who is able to talk of . . . unnecessary points, or even of truths of a lower degree of necessity, how excellent soever, while he seeth a company of ignorant, carnel, miserable sinners before his eyes, who must be changed or damned? . . . O call after the impenitent, and ply this great work of converting souls, whatever else you leave undone."[20] If we compare Herbert to these other Protestants, a strange picture emerges; while Luther, Calvin, and Baxter are looking into their parishioners' eternal destinies, Herbert examines their butteries. How are we to understand such a curious state of affairs?

In religious discourse that places an emphasis on the outer man —his experience, behavior, and appearance—the subject of faith and works can hardly be avoided. In *The Country Parson* we see that it has not been. Although Herbert admits to subscribing to the Anglican catechism and authority (255:16–17; 253:5–9), he comes unusually close to suggesting some sort of efficacy for good works in regard to justification. In "The Parson in Liberty," for example, Herbert submits that a particular prayer regimen is somehow essential for salvation: "It is necessary, that all Christians should pray twice a day, every day of the week, and four times on Sunday, if they be well. This is so necessary, and essentiall to a Christian, that he cannot without this maintain himself in a Christian state" (272:24–25). With this requirement Herbert takes issue with the reformers and his own Church of England. English Protestants up until Herbert's time enjoyed a near consensus regarding the eternal security of the believer.[21] That is, most agreed that a truly converted soul had no fear of losing his place in heaven because of sin committed after conversion. Early on Luther comforted the conscientious believer on this point: "Even when my sins oppress me most, when they gnaw, when they haunt and terrify me, I look to Christ, believe in Him with feeble faith, hold to Him, and say: 'I am assured, for Thou hast said: "He who believes in Me shall have eternal life."' Even though my conscience is troubled, and sin frightens me and makes my heart quake, it is written nonetheless: 'Take heart, my son; your sins are forgiven' (Matt. 9:2); and: 'You shall have everlasting life, and I will raise you up on the Last Day.'"[22] Because salvation, in the Protestant paradigm, depends fundamentally on faith in Christ's work and not on one's own works, a believer's "bad works" will not jeopardize his salvation, although they will certainly hinder his spiritual growth. This is how Calvin could affirm to fellow believers: "we stand by the power of God, lest any doubt arising from a consciousness of our own infirmity, should disquiet us. How weak soever we may then be, yet our salvation is not uncertain, because it is sustained by God's power."[23] Article Seventeen of the Thirty-Nine Articles of the Church of England similarly explains that nothing will interfere with the eventual salvation of the believer: "Predestination to Life is the everlasting purpose of God, whereby (before the foundations of the world were laid) he hath constantly decreed by his counsel, secret to us, to deliver from the curse and damnation those whom he hath chosen in Christ out of mankind, and to bring them Christ to everlasting salvation, as vessels made to honour."[24] Bringing believers to "everlasting salvation" "by Christ" rather than by their own prayers or any other works of their own is the essence of the Protestant doctrine known as "The Perseverance of the Saints." Herbert's warning that without a certain form of prayers a believer cannot "maintain himself in a Christian state" seems strange when compared to mainstream Protestant teaching. Again in *The Country Parson* what one does—his behavior, experiences, or the religious forms he exercises—is given more attention than one's faith in right doctrine.[25]

In chapter 19, "The Parson in reference," Herbert attempts to justify some of this attention to the outer man with a biblical injunction. But he uses Philippians 4:8 in a context different from its original and even changes the wording to suit his purpose. To a persecuted church, Paul wrote Philippians encouraging his readers to strengthen the inner man through prayer and edifying thought. In the Authorized Version (1611) Philippians 4:6–8 reads: "Bee carefull for nothing: but in every thing by prayer and supplication with thankesgiving, let your requests be made knowen unto God. And the peace of God which passeth all understanding, shall keepe your hearts & minds through Christ Jesus. Finally, brethren, whatsoever things are true, whatsoever things are honest, whatsoever things are just, whatsoever things are pure, whatsoever things are lovely, whatsoever things are of good report: if there bee any vertue, and if there bee any praise, thinke on these things." Paul's emphasis is clearly on the inner man, his faith and state of mind. Herbert uses this passage instead to encourage good works, to shape the active, not the contemplative lives of his readers. In an effort to motivate his readers to help their neighbors, Herbert quotes the final part of verse 8 this way: "For the Apostles rule Philip. 4. being admirable and large that *we should do* whatsoever things are honest, or just, or pure, or lovely, or of good report, if there be any vertue, or any praise." Paul wrote "*thinke* on these things." Herbert writes instead "that we should *do* them" (253: 23 my emphasis). Paul's concern was with the hearts and minds of his flock. Herbert's is with their observable behavior. Paul wanted to strengthen his readers' faith, Herbert (apparently) their works.

In "The Parson's Knowledge" (chapter 4), Herbert again adjusts a biblical text to express his concerns regarding doctrine and life, faith and works. Herbert begins with what is an orthodox Protestant explanation of the source of his doctrine: "the chief and top of [the parson's] knowledge consists in the book of books, the storehouse and magazene of life and comfort, the holy Scriptures" (228:21–24). Even in detailing the contents of Scripture, however, Herbert reveals his particular emphasis: "In the Scriptures hee findes four things; Precepts for life, Doctrines for knowledge, Examples for illustration, and Promises for comfort" (228:23–26). The parson finds "precepts for Life" before "doctrines for knowledge." Herbert appears to derive his hermeneutic from what he sees as a scriptural model that makes life in some sense prior to doctrine. He explains: "But for understanding these [precepts, doctrines, examples, and promises in Scripture]; the means he useth are first, a *holy Life,* remembring what his Master saith, that *if any do God's will, he shall know of the Doctrine*, John 7" (228:26–28, my emphasis). This statement seems to be Herbert's biblical justification for his unusual attention to the holy life: a holy life precedes doctrinal understanding. But this ordering turns much of Protestant theology on its head. Here Herbert claims that one cannot come to a proper discernment of the truth without first leading an upright life. Furthermore, by removing a biblical statement from its original context Herbert changes its meaning to make this point. The verse he quotes comes from a passage that the Authorized Version translates: "Now about the midst of the feast Jesus went up into the temple and taught. And the Jews marvelled saying, How knoweth this man letters, having never learned? Jesus answered them and said, My doctrine is not mine, but his that sent me. If any man will to do God's will, he shall know of the doctrine, whether it be of God, or whether I speak of myself" (John 7: 15–17). By taking a sentence out of the narrative without the final clause Herbert effectively shifts the meaning of the biblical passage. In their context these words are an effort to establish the identity of Jesus and the authority of his teaching ("My doctrine is not mine, but his that sent me.") But for Herbert, Jesus' words are used to support the claim that to understand precepts and doctrines in Scripture, one must first lead a holy life. For Herbert verse seventeen becomes a general hermeneutical rule: *Do* God's will in order to know the doctrine.

This use of John 7 becomes even more significant when we remember that Herbert undoubtedly knew Greek.[26] A Greek transliteration of John 7:17 reads: "If anyone wishes the will of him to do, he will know concerning the teaching, whether of God it is or I from myself speak."[27] The Greek word θέλη ("wishes") certainly softens the verse's demand. One who *wishes* to do God's will—even if he does not or cannot—shall know if Jesus' teachings are from God. One need not actually be holy, Jesus is saying, but simply willing to "know of the doctrine." Herbert could have easily chosen another rendering of the verse. Both Luther and Calvin had before him. Luther translated the verse: "If any man's will is to do His will . . . "[28] and Calvin: "If any man willith to do his will."[29] Herbert's choice is more demanding than either the original Greek or his Protestant forbearers would require.

He holds that one must already be obedient to God in living a holy life in order to know the truth: "if any man *do* God's will, he shall know of the doctrine" (228:28, my emphasis). Traditionally Protestants have argued rather that one needs to know the truth in order to be obedient; that is, one must be a believer in the truth ("regenerate" or "converted") in order to be able to obey the truth. Herbert seems to suggest that obedience somehow precedes faith or understanding.

The reformers taught that before men are set free by the true doctrine, they cannot be obedient, but are slaves to sin. Faith in true doctrine, the Gospel, releases one from this bondage and enables him to live righteously. Calvin explains: "it is clear that by nature we are the slaves of sin . . . But when the Lord regenerates us by His Spirit He also makes us free, so that we are released from the snares of Satan and willingly obey righteousness. But regeneration comes from faith. Hence it is evident that freedom is from the Gospel."[30] While the reformers insisted that faith in true doctrine is prerequisite to holy living, Herbert suggests that true doctrine cannot be understood without a holy life. A conflict seems to exist between Herbert and his spiritual forefathers. There also seems to be tension between Herbert and the Church of England on this point. Like the reformers, the church taught that before one is justified by faith in true doctrine, none of his "good" works are acceptable to God because before one is regenerate none of his works are really good. Article 13 of the *Thirty-Nine Articles* (1571) states: "Works done before the grace of Christ, and the inspiration of his Spirit, are not pleasant to God, forasmuch as they spring not out of faith in Jesus Christ, neither do they make men meet to receive grace, or (as the school authors say) deserve grace of congruity: yea rather, for that they are not done as God hath willed and commanded them to be done, we doubt not but they have the nature of sin."[31]

The *Thirty-Nine Articles* state that there is no holy living prior to holy belief. But Herbert breaks with the *Articles* on this point as he does with the reformers and contemporary Protestant interpretations of the scriptures themselves. Throughout *The Country Parson* Herbert departs from traditional Protestant trends. Specifically, in *The Country Parson* Herbert emphasizes life over doctrine, the outer man over the inner, and works over faith.[32] When compared to other contemporary clerical manuals, *The Country Parson* stands apart. Comparisons and suggestions for *The Country Parson*'s unique strategies and purposes are the subjects of the following chapters.

2
The Country Parson and Contemporary Clerical Manuals

I joy, deare Mother, when I view
Thy perfect lineaments, and hue
        Both sweet and bright.
Beautie in thee takes up her place,
And dates her letters from thy face,
        When she doth write.
A fine aspect in fit aray,
Neither too mean, nor yet too gay,
        Shows who is best.
Outlandish looks may not compare:
For all they either painted are,
        Or else undrest.
She on the hills, which wantonly
Allureth all in hope to be
        By her preferr'd,
Hath kiss'd so long her painted shrines,
That ev'n her face by kissing shines,
        For her reward.
She in the valley is so shie
Of dressing, that her hair doth lie
        About her eares:
While she avoids her neighbours pride,
She wholly goes on th'other side,
        And nothing wears.
But, dearest Mother, what those misse,
The mean, thy praise and glorie is,
        And long may be.

Blessed be God, whose love it was
To double-moat thee with his grace,
And none but thee.
—George Herbert
"The British Church"

THE SURPRISING LITERARY AND THEOLOGICAL CHOICES IN HERBERT'S *The Country Parson* may perhaps be made more intelligible by an understanding of the context in which Herbert was writing. The actual Church of England—unlike the serene picture of her in Herbert's poem—was experiencing an internal conflict of immense proportions, a conflict in which, whether or not Herbert willed it, his own works were destined to take part.

From the moment of publication, *The Temple* and *The Country Parson* were admired by Puritan and Anglo-Catholic alike: "Everyone seemed to love Herbert's poetry, and many claimed him as a posthumous ally. Herbert was no less an inspiration for the Puritan expatriate Edward Taylor than for the Anglican Henry Vaughan, and many devout English Puritans embraced him."[1] Barnabas Oley, who first published *Herbert's Remains* in 1652, seems to have believed Herbert a firm Laudian and retitled *The Country Parson* as *A Priest to the Temple*.[2] Richard Baxter gave Herbert high Puritan praise: "Herbert speaks to God like one that really believeth a God, and which business in the world is most with God. Heart-work and Heaven work make up his Books."[3] Low Churchmen were attracted by Herbert's piety which they took as natural to the Reformed tradition. High Churchmen appreciated Herbert's love of form, ceremony, and the sacraments, and attributed this disposition to an Anglo-Catholic heritage.[4]

The question of Herbert's inspiration and allegiance persists. Modern critics still often claim Herbert for one camp or the other. Rosemond Tuve, Louis Martz, Stanley Stewart, among others, trace Herbert's muse to medieval and Catholic origins, while William Halewood, Joseph Summers, Richard Strier, Barbara Lewalski and others explain that the sources informing Herbert's genius are chiefly Protestant and even Puritan.[5] Some critics conclude that we will never know where Herbert's deepest loyalties and literary debts lay. They correctly point out that

Herbert died before Archbishop Laud came into power, and thus was never forced to expose his profoundest commitments. Many of Herbert's critics ignore altogether this knotty question of convictions. They suggest instead that Herbert was apolitical, since to choose any side of the religious debates in seventeenth-century England was to make a political statement, and they emphasize the elements in Herbert's work of universal appeal, which transcend partisan bickering.

While it is true that Herbert's appeal was and is universal, the apolitical position is least fair to Herbert himself. Herbert in fact did take an interest in the controversies of the time. In a letter to his stepfather, Sir John Danvers, Herbert asks for money to acquire "those infinite Volumes of Divinity, which yet every day swell, and grow bigger" (365:14–15). Ilona Bell comments on that request this way: "His interest in these swelling and growing volumes suggests that he was anxiously keeping up with the burgeoning arguments of Calvinists, Puritans, and Anglo-Catholics, all substantial and vocal parties in the pre-Laudian Church. In writing the Latin poems *Musae Responsoriae*, Herbert even entered the fray for a short time. He was intellectually sophisticated, theologically curious, and politically ambitious."[6]

Herbert was indeed "intellectually sophisticated," "theologically curious," and politically concerned. We are not wholly uncertain regarding his particular religious/political views. While Herbert's poetry evidences both Anglo-Catholic and Puritan loyalties, *The Country Parson* provides a clearer message. Here Herbert puts forth a politically impossible, yet personally satisfying, third alternative: a middle way. Herbert's desire to take what he viewed as the best of the different trends within the church may begin to explain his universal appeal. Further, it sheds light on his apparent preferences in *The Country Parson* for "life" over doctrine, the outer man over the inner, and works over faith.

Herbert's effort to steer a middle course between the Genevan and Roman traditions is especially evident in his poem, "The British Church." Here he depicts the Church of England ideally as "double-moated" against the errors of both Roman Catholic and Reformed parties. Using a metaphor of appearances, Herbert explains that the British Church's beauty comes from striking a balance: "Neither too mean, nor yet too gay, / Shows who is best." The Roman Catholic Church ("She on the hills, which wantonly / Allureth all . . . ") he depicts in traditional polemics as the Whore of Babylon, while the Genevan Church he describes as plain and even careless about her looks: "She in the valley is so shie / Of dressing, that her hair doth lie / About her eares." The Church of England alone strikes a proper balance: "The mean thy praise and glory is."

Yet in another poem, "The Church Militant," Herbert shows himself critical of the Anglo-Catholic establishment and truly sympathetic to the separatist cause:

> Religion stands on tip-toe in our land,
> Readie to passe to the *American* strand . . .
> (196:235–36)

> Whereby one may foretell, what sinnes next yeare
> Shall both in *France* and *England* domineer:
> Then shall Religion to *America* flee:
> They have their times of Gospel, ev'n as we.
> (197:245–48)

For Herbert, in many senses, the ideal Church of England is a compromise, a balance between the Reformed and Roman Catholic traditions. In reality, true religion "stands on tip-toe in our land / Readie to passe" with the Puritans to the New World. *The Country Parson* is Herbert's attempt to help the British Church be in reality more like the ideal. In the person of the model country parson, Herbert unites the best of the Anglo-Catholic and Puritan traditions.

That Herbert was aware of the appeal for the typical Anglican of the larger Catholic and Protestant communities is evident from chapter 24, "The Parson arguing." It is significant that of all the confusions and heresies the parson might be called upon to address in such a chapter, Herbert chooses only two: papacy and schismaticism. His perfect parson must resist the immoderate appeals from both sides and teach his people to do the same. Quite obviously, Herbert's greatest doctrinal arguments are with those within the Anglican Church who take their partisanship to the extreme.[7] In the case of Anglo-Catholics the unacceptable extreme is papal allegiance; in that of the Puritans, it is separatism. In a way that reveals his own preference for a "middle way," Herbert suggests reasoning with both parties:

> if he be a Papist, the Church is the hinge he turnes on; if a Schismatick, scandall. Wherefore the Parson hath diligently examined these two with himselfe, as what the Church is, how it began, how it proceeded, whether it be a rule to it selfe, whether it hath a rule, whether having a rule, it ought not to be guided by it; whether any rule in the world be obscure, and how then should the best be so, at least in fundamentall things, the obscurity in some points being the exercise of the Church, the light in the foundations being the guide; The Church needing both an evidence, and an exercise. So for Scandall: what scandall is, when given or taken; whether, there being two precepts, one of obeying Authority, the other of not giving scandall, that ought not to be preferred, especially since in disobeying there is scandall also; whether things once indifferent, being made by the precept of Authority more then indifferent, it be in our power to omit or refuse them. (262:29–63:14)

This passage demonstrates Herbert's loyalty to the Anglican Church as the *via media* between Roman Catholicism and radical Protestantism. It shows Herbert's commitment to the primary distinctive of Protestantism, scripture's authority over the church: the church "having a rule" (that is, scripture), it ought to "be guided by it." At the same time the passage expresses Herbert's rejection of the extremist Protestant position in which the church has no authority over things "indifferent," that is, things not specifically sanctioned by scripture, like the various ceremonies of the Church of England. Herbert maintains that when "things once indifferent [are] made by the precept of Authority more than indifferent," it is no longer "in our power to omit or refuse them." As one dedicated to the ideal of the Anglican *via media*, Herbert insists that while the church has authority where scripture is silent or confusing, scripture exercises authority over the church in every other area.[8]

Herbert seeks the middle way in practical as well as theological issues. In "The Parson preaching" (232–35) and "The Parson's Knowledge" (228–29) he borrows alternatively from contemporary Puritan and Anglo-Catholic practices. We have already noted (in chapter 1) how Herbert, in a very non-Puritan fashion, devotes only a small part of his chapter on preaching to actual explication of the biblical text. Instead, he addresses most of "The Parson preaching" to sermon delivery and pulpit appearances. However, when Herbert does get to the sermon itself he praises the Puritan plain style and criticizes the sermon style most often associated with High churchmen: "The Parson's Method in handling of a text consists of two parts; first, a plain and evident declaration of the meaning of the text; and secondly, some choyce Observations drawn out of the whole text, as it lyes entire, and unbroken in Scripture it self. This he thinks naturall, and sweet, and grave. Whereas the other way of crumbling a text into small parts, as, the Person speaking, or spoken to, the subject, and object, and the like, hath neither in it sweetnesse, nor gravity, nor variety, since the words apart are not Scripture, but a dictionary, and may be considered alike in all the Scripture" (234:36–35:10).

In his day Herbert's approbation of "plain" sermonizing would have been immediately recognized as a Puritan value. William Perkins, the famous Puritan spokesman for the plain sermon writes, "Here first we are to observe the properties of the Ministry of the Word. The first, that it must bee plaine, perspicuous, and evident . . . It is a by-word among us: *It was a very* plaine Sermon: And I say againe, *the plainer, the better*."[9] Despite the disagreement among critics as to what elements exactly distinguish the Anglo-Catholic's sermon, all agree on the Puritan fervor for the plain style. Charles and Katherine George, normally skeptical that any real differences existed between Puritans and other Anglicans, write: "[A] fairly clear monopoly of 'puritan' divines is the formulation and publicizing, as an ideal for the good minister, of that style of preaching which is . . . designated by its champions as 'plain.'"[10] Thus, when he calls for a "plain and evident declaration of the text," Herbert approves of the Puritan sermon style. The "other way of crumbling a text into small parts," which Herbert clearly disapproves, is associated most with Anglo-Catholic divines. W. Fraser Mitchell explains that explicating by discovering "the subject, and object, and the like," was common to High Churchmen, and he provides two famous examples: "Minute attendance to cases or parts of speech . . .

may be gathered from the work of Andrewes and Donne."[11] Perry Miller distinguishes the two sermon styles that existed in both Old and New World Anglican churches: "before the 1640's . . . there were two opposed theories of form, style and function of the sermon which were identified with the two parties most radically opposed in theology and ecclesiastical doctrine . . . To compare a sermon of Andrewes or of Donne with one of Cotton or of Hooker is to see at a glance the fundamental points of contrast; the difference of form is pronounced, for the Anglican sermon is much more an oration, much closer to classical and patristic eloquence, while the Puritan work . . . appears on the printed page more like a lawyer's brief than a work of art."[12]

The Anglo-Catholics were famous for their wit, conceits, and displays of classical learning. The Puritan, while often just as well educated as any Laudian, wasted no effort on "ornamenting" his text because for the Puritan the purpose of preaching was first and foremost "to sink the abstract doctrine into the minds of listeners."[13] When Herbert describes his ideal parson as "not witty, or learned, or eloquent but Holy" he is placing himself among the Puritans. Miller argues, "Sermon style was not a matter of taste and preference, it was a party badge."[14]

In sermon preparation as well as style Herbert shows himself quite at home with practices commonly associated with the Puritans. In "The Parsons Knowledg," where Herbert exposes his biblical hermeneutic, we find an unabashed confidence in the individual's ability to discern truth privately with only his own heart and the help of the Holy Spirit. Here Herbert puts his conscience and his own meditations on the same level with those of the Church Fathers:

> The . . . Commenters and Fathers . . . have handled the places controverted, which the Parson by no means refuseth. *As he doth not so study others as to neglect the grace of God in himself, and what the Holy Spirit teacheth him so doth he assure himself, that God in all ages hath had his servants, to whom he hath revealed his Truth, as well as to him* and that as one Countrey doth not bear all things, that there may be a Commerce; so neither hath God opened, or will open all to one, that there may be a traffick in knowledg between the servants of God, for the planting both of love, and humility. Wherfore he hath one Comment at least upon every book of Scripture, and ploughing with this, *and his*

own meditations, he enters into the secrets of God treasured in the holy Scripture. (229:17–30, my emphasis)

It certainly would be unfair to suggest that the Anglo-Catholic preacher did not depend upon the help of the Holy Spirit to guide him in his study of scripture. Nevertheless, we rarely see this sort of confidence in God's revelation to the individual expressed outside of Puritan writings. One of the distinguishing marks of the Puritan movement was its pious individualism. While the Puritans did not go as far as some enthusiasts did in exalting private revelation above the scriptures and Church tradition, "All [Puritans] believed that every man could come to know God in his own heart and in the word, that the inner voice of conscience was the voice of God."[15] On this point, however, Herbert does not unequivocally take sides. He desires a middle way; the parson studies the "grace of God in himself," and the Fathers, "what the Holy Spirit teacheth him," and the "Commenters"; he "ploughs" with "his own meditations, and the ancients." We rarely find such attention to private promptings of the Spirit among High Church authors. Herbert chooses the middle path both doctrinally and homiletically.

Herbert's mediating spirit appears again in his description of "The Parson's Church," chapter 13. After going into great detail regarding the appearance of nearly every utensil and piece of furniture in the building, Herbert makes clear his motives for such lavish attention to church fixtures. His explanation is a mediating one:

> And all this he doth, not as out of necessity, or as putting a holiness in the things, but as *desiring to keep a middle way between superstition, and slovenlinesse*, and as following the Apostles two great and admirable Rules in things of this nature: The first whereof is, Let all things be done decently, and in order: The second, Let all things be done to edification, I Corinthians 14. For these two rules comprize and include the double object of our duty, God, and our neighbour; the first being for the honour of God; the second for the benefit of our neighbor. So that they excellently score out the way, and fully, and exactly contain, even in externall and indifferent things, what course is to be taken; and put them to great shame, who deny the Scripture to be perfect. (246:22–47:2, my emphasis)

Herbert's desire "to keep the middle way between superstition, and slovinlinesse" is clearly a desire to avoid what was seen as the excesses of the Roman and Genevan traditions. In Herbert's day "superstitious" was a common term of derision describing the Roman Catholic Church. In several places in *The Country Parson* Herbert uses the term himself while obviously referring to Roman practices, as for example: "In the time of Popery, the Priests Benedicite, and his holy water were over valued; and now we are fallen to the clean contrary, even from superstition to coldnes, and Atheism" (286:15–18, see also 273:21–23 and 284:28–29).

"Superstition" or "putting a holiness in the things" is Herbert's Roman Scylla. The Puritan or Reformed Charybdis is "slovinlinesse," not caring enough about the appearance of things, as in Herbert's depiction of the Reformed congregations in "The British Church." There Herbert describes them as a woman "shei of dressing," with her hair lying "about her eares." He finds the Reformed Communion too "mean" and bare: "She wholly goes on th' other side, /And nothing wears." Herbert continues in this vein in "The Parson's Church" and gives scriptural sanction for his middle way. To care about appearances is the opposite of slovenliness; it is to honor God and to do things "decently." But caring about appearances must not become excessive or "superstitious"; it must always be "for the benefit of our neighbor" and "done to edification." Worshipping God both "decently" and "to edification" are commanded by the Apostle Paul in I Corinthians 14. Regarding the church and its ceremonial accouterments, then, Herbert wants to combine the aesthetic with the edifying, the Roman concern with outward appearances and the Genevan emphasis on inner realities and spiritual growth.

We have noted three ways in which Herbert's country parson embodies his vision for the Anglican church as a *via media*: doctrinally ("The Parson arguing"), in his preaching and biblical exegesis ("The Parson preaching" and "The Parson's Knowledg") and in matters of appearances and ceremonial significance ("The Parson's Church"). Herbert shows himself amenable to practices of both parties in these areas. These three passages comprise the most straightforward textual evidence for Herbert's moderating thrust in *The Country Parson*. By examining other clerical manuals of the same period we will find still more reasons to believe that the ideal country parson was Herbert's attempt to elicit the best from different factions within the church. Among the manuals to which we shall make reference, William Perkins's *Of the Calling of the Ministrie*[16] and Richard Bernard's *The Faithfull Shepheard*[17] deserve a special introduction because of the important role they played in the contemporary church and perhaps in motivating Herbert's own writing.

William Perkins (1558–1602) and Richard Bernard (1568–1641) were well known as Puritans in their day. Perkins was famous for the vehement stance he took against all High Church rituals that savored of Romanism.[18] His treatise, *Reformed Catholic* (1597), delineating the differences of Catholic and Protestant doctrine, "continued to be studied throughout the seventeenth century as an authority but little inferior to Hooker or Calvin."[19] Richard Bernard, too, balked against High Church practices and wrote prodigiously for the Puritan cause, including one biting attack called *Twelve Arguments proving that the Ceremonies imposed upon the ministers of England by the Prelates are unlawful*. But neither Perkins nor Bernard was a fringe fanatic. They were Anglicans of the Puritan party or "brotherhood," and what they hoped to bring to pass were changes within, not separate from, the Church of England. Bernard, in fact, wrote a tract entitled, *Plain Evidences the Church of England is Apostolicall, the Separation, Schismaticall* (1610),[20] and Perkins is quoted as saying, "those that make a separation from our Church because of corruption in it are far from the spirit of Christ and his Apostles."[21] So when we read the pastoral advice given by these authors, we are not reading wild, separatist propaganda, but the wishes of loyal, albeit dissatisfied, members of the Church of England.

Perkins and Bernard belonged to an informal group of Puritan preachers who banded together for mutual support and influence, which included Laurence Chaderton, Arthur Hildersam, John Dod, and later John Cotton, Richard Sibbes, John Preston, and Thomas Shepard.[22] They all shared a hostility toward the "weak hearts" and "men pleasers" who failed to "perform the work of the ministry as (they) ought."[23] Called the "Spiritual

Brotherhood," their chief aim was to reshape the English ministry toward what they saw as a more scriptural and Reformed discipline. David D. Hall summarizes their program this way:

> The organizers of the brotherhood were men who shared with Calvin and John Hooper the ideal of a highly trained, zealous corps of preachers, men the opposite in every way of the "dumb dogs" and "loose livers" presently installed within the church. To recruit and train these zealous preachers was a business that the organizers of the brotherhood could only carry on in ways that did not challenge the authority of church and crown. Denied the freedom to have independent schools . . . members of the brotherhood took control of certain common rooms: Christ's College, Cambridge, while Perkins was alive, and Emmanuel, which Laurence Chaderton directed from its founding in 1584. Outside the universities older members of the brotherhood carried on the training of graduates in household seminaries. To supplement these forms of acculturation the group produced its own books of discipline, a literature that included Perkins's Of the Calling of the Ministry and Bernard's The Faithfull Shepherd. As a final measure there began to appear the "spiritual biographies" of ministers who exemplified an ideal type.[24]

To some, parts of this brotherhood seemed to move in an extreme direction. What Herbert loved about his church, and what all others missed in his opinion, was the way she remained free from the errors of extremism: "But dearest Mother, (what those misse) / The mean thy praise and glorie is." It should not be surprising then that when he saw other members of the British Church vehemently agitating for change in one direction, Herbert should want to do his part in providing a corrective. *The Country Parson* may be just such a corrective to the wave of Puritan sentiment of the day. With *The Country Parson* Herbert meant to balance the scales, to offer a much needed alternative to the Puritan dominated genre.

The most outstanding difference between *The Country Parson* and most other clerical manuals has to do with what they say about the spiritual state of the minister himself. We have already seen (chapter 1) how Herbert focuses on the outer appearances instead of the inner man. This emphasis in *The Country Parson* becomes even more striking as we observe the overriding concern among other manual writers for the inner state of their subjects.

Perkins begins his treatise with a quotation from the Book of Job: "If there bee with him a Messenger: An Interpreter, one of a thousand to declare unto man his righteousnes: Then will [God] have mercy on him, and will say, deliver him that hee goe not downe into the pit, for I have received a reconciliation" (Job 33:23–24). Perkins clarifies that the Messenger or Interpreter in these verses is a minister of the Gospel. But before he fully explains how the minister is to "declare unto man his righteousness" (i.e., through faith in Jesus Christ), Perkins insists that the minister himself be reconciled to God: "God hateth him which will take in hand to reconcile others, himselfe beeing unreconciled to God. Seeing then Ministers are Gods Interpreters to the people to declare and publish their reconciliation with God . . . let therefore all true ministers of God: first be Gods Interpreters to their owne consciences and their souls."[25] Perkins urgently asks these questions regarding the would-be minister: "A Minister is to declare the reconciliation betwixt God and man, and is he himselfe not reconciled? Dare he present another man to Gods mercy for pardon, and never yet presented himselfe: Can hee commend the state of Grace to another, & never felt the sweetnes thereof in his owne soule? Dare hee come to preach sanctification with polluted lyps, and out of an unsanctified hart?"[26]

The preacher's own reconciliation with God, or salvation, is a point of great concern to the Puritan authors. Richard Baxter writes in the opening lines of *The Reformed Pastor*: "See that the work of saving grace be thoroughly wrought in your own souls. Take heed to yourselves, brethren, lest you should be destitute of that saving grace of God which you offer to others, and be strangers to the effectual working of that gospel which you preach."[27]

Baxter wants to make clear that no outward appearances of godliness, not even the clerical collar, but only a right inner state, can save a man: "Can any reasonable man imagine, that God should save men for offering salvation to others while they refused it themselves; and for telling others those truths which they themselves neglected and abused? . . . Believe it, brethren,

God never saved any man for being a preacher, nor because he was a preacher; but because he was a justified, sanctified man."[28]

While the Puritan divines continually insist upon the need for the pastor to be sure of his salvation, Herbert is completely silent on the subject. Other authors' first concern is to be sure of the minister's faith. For Herbert, this seems to be no issue whatsoever.

One explanation for Herbert's silence, of course, might be that Herbert did not care at all about the state of his ideal pastor's soul. If articulated concern were the only measuring stick, we might conclude that Herbert indeed demonstrates a shocking indifference toward the ultimate fate of his country parson. But the more likely explanation for his silence is that Herbert assumes the parson already to be in a state of grace, that is, to be a true believer. Unlike his fellow handbook authors, Herbert feels no need to cry out against unbelieving clergy. He expresses no fears like Baxter's that a clergyman might be "destitute of that saving grace of God" that he offers to others. That Herbert assumes the parson to be a dedicated Christian is evident from statements like this one: "The Countrey Parson is generally sad, because hee knows nothing but the Crosse of Christ, his mind being defixed on it with those nailes wherewith his Master was" (267:27–30). Such a disposition surely belongs to a true believer. Although Herbert never specifies that the ideal parson must be a thoroughly converted man, passages like this one suggest that he assumed such a converted state. The Puritan Brotherhood, on the other hand, with their particular understanding of conversion, would never think of making such an assumption.

While all English Protestants agreed to the need for conversion, "Puritans placed a great deal more emphasis upon the urgency of a sincere conviction of sin and repentance than Anglicans did."[29] The "most striking difference of emphasis between the Anglican and Puritan explications of the doctrine of justification," J. Sears McGee writes, "is also the most relative. Simply stated it is that Puritans made it sound hard, and Anglicans made it sound easy."[30] The two parties in Herbert's day were quite aware of this distinction. The Puritan Richard Sibbes sarcastically condemned those "base men, that live in the church," but "turn over all religion to a 'Lord have mercy upon us, and

Christ died for us,' and 'we hope we have souls to God-ward.'" Conversely, the Anglican, Humphrey Sydenham pleaded with Puritans to replace the "rough dialect of the law; horror, blood and death" with "the sweet language of the Gospel, brethren, and beseeching, and mercies of God."[31] By never mentioning the hard way of conversion and simply assuming the justification of the parson, on this issue Herbert's work clearly falls to the High Church or Anglican side. Among "advices to clergy" Herbert's manual is unusual in this regard.

The Country Parson further stands out among clerical manuals in that it does not assume, like most others do, that the parson desperately needs to search his heart for sin undoubtedly lurking there. Not only is the salvation of the minister in question for other manual authors but his sanctification (that is, his progress in the faith) is as well. In fact, most writers make the pastor's own spiritual growth a central concern of their treatises.

While Herbert rarely touches on the parson's feelings and only in passing mentions his conscience, other divines see these faculties as real indicators of spiritual health. They encourage examination of the emotions and conscience. Richard Baxter, for example, writes "If it be not your daily business to study your own hearts . . . all will go wrong,"[32] and he warns ministers to heed the voice of conscience because: "If our hearts condemn us, God is greater than our hearts, and will condemn us much more."[33] Perkins, too, exhorts students in divinity to gain courage for their vocation by prayer and self-examination: "Let that man set himselfe in Gods presence, enter into himselfe, search his conscience, finde out his sinnes, confesse and bewayle them to God, crave pardon in Christes blood, and grace to leave them, and cease not till hee heare the voyce of Gods spirit sounding in his conscience: THY SINNES ARE FORGIVEN THEE."[34]

While Herbert never demands such introspection, Gilbert Burnet asks of carnal ministers by way of warning: "what confidence can they have in God, when their own consciences will reproach them?"[35]

But if their own consciences will not reproach the clergyman, the Puritan authors do their best to stir up a sense of spiritual need with their handbooks. While Herbert will rarely—if, in fact, ever—reproach his readers, the accusatorial tone is common among other manual authors. Perkins, for example, asks this condemning question of fellow clergymen: "how canst thou be a true witnes to testifie betwixt God, and the soule of a sinner, when thy owne soule knoweth not, nor feeleth the truth of it?"[36] Burnet laments, "If men had the spirit of their calling in them, and a due measure of flame and heat in carrying it on; labour in it would be rather a pleasure than a trouble."[37] And Baxter, with his usual passion accuses and pleads: "Alas, in our hearts, as well as in our hearers, there are an averseness to God—a strangeness to him—unreasonable, and almost unruly passions. In us there are, at the best, the remnants of pride, unbelief, selfishness, hypocrisy, and all the most hateful, deadly sins And doth it not, then, concern us to take heed to ourselves?"[38] "Take heed to ourselves"—this is the heartbeat of Puritan clerical handbooks. The heartbeat of Herbert's work, however, is "Take heed to the flock." While most Puritan authors take their focus inward, on the pastor's own heart and fitness to preach the gospel, Herbert's focus is away from the parson's heart, onto his public image and his efficacy among his people. And while most authors concentrate heavily upon the parson's heart, Herbert concentrates on his behavior and fittingly defines the minister in terms of action: "Out of this Chartre of the Priesthood may be plainly gathered both the Dignity and the Duty: The Dignity, in that a Priest may *do* that which Christ did, and by his authority, and as his Viceregent. The Duty, in that a Priest is *to do* that which Christ did, and after his manner, both for Doctrine and Life (225:14–19, my italics)."[39]

This difference between Herbert and the Puritan manual authors gets at the root of the distinction between seventeenth-century Anglo-Catholics and Puritans. Many different models have been created to describe the High Church/Low Church or Anglo-Catholic/Puritan relationship. One particularly helpful one is described by J. Sears McGee in his book, *The Godly Man in Stuart England: Anglicans, Puritans, and the Two Tables, 1620–1670.* The "Two Tables" are the tablets of the Ten Commandments. McGee writes: "Although the accounts in the Old Testament do not say which laws were on which tablets, tradition dictated that the first four (which express man's duties to God) appeared on the First Table. The latter six (which describe man's duties to other men) were engraved on the Second Table. The distinction between the two was a widely used device in catechisms and summaries of Christian doctrine."[40]

McGee argues that the important distinctions between Puritans and the rest of the Anglicans can be summed up best by their respective attitudes toward each of the Two Tables. He suggests: "The performance of duties toward God and man was essential for both Anglicans and Puritans. The point is rather that, by comparison, the Puritans tended to emphasize the First Table more heavily and to make it a touchstone to the Second."[41] And of the Anglo-Catholics McGee writes: "In terms of emphasis, Anglicans reversed the relationship between the two tables of the Ten Commandments. They made the Second Table duties the touchstone to the First."[42]

This characterization might lead one to conclude that the Puritans were more strictly "reformed" than the Anglicans because the Puritans put their duty toward God (i.e., faith) over their duty toward their fellow man (i.e., good works) while the Anglicans seemed to have the opposite priority. Undoubtedly the Puritans of the time concluded thus. But McGee explains how the Anglicans were able apparently to take their First Table duties for granted: "They could do this because they believed that the Church of England was not, as the Puritans thought, an ugly caterpillar struggling toward the exquisite completeness of the butterfly, but rather a liturgically beautiful and spiritually satisfying offspring of the travail of the Reformation in England."[43]

That is, because of their high view of the Church of England, Anglicans were able to trust that their First Table responsibilities toward God were sufficiently performed as they participated properly and sincerely in the rites of the church. Since their First Table duties were thus fulfilled, they could concentrate unreservedly upon performing good works among their fellow men: "Anglicans regarded the First Table requirements as entirely fulfilled by honest participation in the prescribed rituals and [believed] that . . . the mark of a good Christian was avoidance of theological controversy and concentration upon Second Table duties."[44]

A Puritan, on the other hand, could never leave to the Church such an important matter as his justification and go on to consider good works or sanctification. Sanctification was rarely even spoken of as an issue separate from justification among Puritans. Instead, sanctification was almost exclusively considered as a proof or assurance of one's conversion. As a typical example of this position, Thomas Watson wrote: "election is the cause of our salvation, sanctification is our evidence. Sanctification is the earmark of Christ's elect sheep."[45]

Herbert, however, writing an Anglican response to the Puritan clerical manual, can accept as given matters of agonizing importance to the Puritans: questions of the minister's salvation and sanctification. Herbert assumed the pastor already to be a mature believer and so concentrated upon improving his behavior instead of his beliefs. This partially explains Herbert's tendency in *The Country Parson* of encouraging the parson toward "good works" while saying very little about his faith.

The Country Parson thus offered a view of the minister that contrasted significantly with that of other clerical handbooks of its time. Not only did Herbert's view of the minister provide a counterpoise, his thoughts on the nature of the ministry also reflected positions contrasting those of the Puritans. Specifically, Herbert's views concerning the purpose, the priorities, and the appearances of the ministry responded to opposing trends in the typical ministerial handbook.

In chapter 1 we found in *The Country Parson* a surprising emphasis on the outward behavior of both parson and congregation. Herbert's understanding of the ministry in part explains such an emphasis. In his opening sentence Herbert defines the purpose of the ministry: "A Pastor is the Deputy of Christ for the reducing of Man to the Obedience of God" (225:1–2). Herbert's parson is especially attentive to the works of his people because the clergyman's very purpose is to help them to obedience. His definition of the vocation ostensibly involves the parishioners' behavior, not their faith. And while Herbert seems to view the purpose of ministry primarily in terms of good works, the Puritans view the purpose of ministry primarily in terms of faith.

Herbert's habit of looking into his parishioners' butteries, examining their bookshelves, and listening to their language before concerning himself with what they believe (e.g., 251:15) provides an unmistakable contrast with the purpose unrelentingly stressed by our other authors: conversion. Rather than "reducing men to the obedience of God," Richard Baxter insists that the purpose of the ministry must be converting the unconverted: "We must labor, in a special manner, FOR THE CONVERSION OF THE UNCONVERTED. The work of conversion is the great thing we must drive at; after this we must labor with all our might."[46] Baxter explains why he emphasizes this task over concern for his parishioners' behavior: "Alas, the misery of the unconverted is so great, that it calleth loudest to us for compassion. If a truly converted sinner do fall, it will be but into sin which will be pardoned, and he is not in that hazard of damnation as others are . . . It is so sad a case to see men in a state of damnation, wherein if they should die, they are lost for ever, that methinks we should not be able to let them alone, either in public or private, whatever other work we have to do."[47]

Like Baxter, Richard Bernard in *The Faithfull Shepheard* describes the purpose of the ministry in terms of faith rather than works. Here he urges those contemplating the ministry to focus on bringing new members into the Body of Christ: "Let true zeale moove thee for Gods glorie, the advancing of Christs kingdome, to convert sinners, and to build the bodie of Christ, to open the eies of the blinde, and to turne them from darknesse to light from Satan unto God."[48] Gilbert Burnet, too, makes compassion for the lost the foremost prerequisite for the ministry. In his opinion those qualities necessary for "an able minister" include "a concern for the souls of men, a tenderness for them, a zeal to rescue them from endless misery, and a desire to put them in the way to everlasting happiness."[49] William Perkins explains the purpose of the ministry this way: "let all Ministers propounde to themselves above all things, THE CONVERSION OF SOULES,"[50] and again, "let us remember the end we aime at is not humane, nor carnall: our purpose is to save soules."[51]

Compared with these authors, George Herbert is conspicuously silent on the topic of conversion. The Puritans' agonized pleas for conversion are matched in Herbert with cool utilitarian suggestions for improving the behavior of parishoners: "So the Countrey Parson . . . sets up as many encouragements to goodnesse as he can, both in honour, and profit, and fame; that he may, if not the best way, yet any way, make his Parish good"

(244:1–5). Herbert's view of the ministry's purpose thus stands in stark contrast with that of other contemporary authors.

An author's views of the purpose of the ministry determine what he sees as the priorities of the ministry. Not surprisingly, Herbert's priorities (as we found them in chapter 1) contrast significantly with those of the Puritan authors. William Perkins quotes Acts 20:21:

"In the Acts, Paule saith of himselfe, that he witnessed to the Jewes, & to the Gentiles, the repentance towards God, and fayth toward our Lord Jesus Christ." From this verse Perkins derives the priorities of the ministry: "first, to preach repentance . . . secondly to preach faith in Christ."[52] For Perkins, as well as for most Puritans, preaching was the chief priority of the minister and the best way to fulfill the ministry's purpose of conversion: "Some preach for feare of the law, to avoyd censure of punishment, some for fashion sake, that they may be like to others, some for ostentation sake, to win credite and prayse, some for ambition to rise in the world: all these forget theyr commission, which is, DELIVER HIM FROM HELL."[53]

No other duty of the minister was as important to the Puritans as preaching. Perkins makes clear that a minister who does not preach misses the central responsibility of his calling: "they therefore are greatly deceived, who thinke a Minister to discharge sufficiently his duetie, though hee preach not, if hee keepe good Hospitalitie and make peace amongst his Neighbours, and performe other workes of charitie and good life: for if a Minister have not this vertue, hee hath none . . . If hee preach not . . . hee hath no conscience, nor can have any comfort, for that is the principall dutie of a Minister."[54]

Richard Bernard, too, believes the minister's chief duty to be preaching. The table of contents to *The Faithfull Shepheard* is a testimony to the primacy of the sermon among these authors; the first three chapters deal in a general way with the minister and the ministry while chapters 4 through 12 are exclusively devoted to the sermon, its preparation and application. Bernard begins his ministerial treatise with an apology for preaching in which he shows preaching to bear a crucial role in salvation history: "When the World by wisdome knew not God in the wisedome of God, it pleased God to appoint a weake meanes, in carnall judgement, even the foolishnesse of preaching to save his elect: And heerein ordinarily God will shew his power to save all that shall be saved. It was from the beginning Preaching and Prophecying, before the fall and after. In Paradise God taught Adam and Eve."[55]

Bernard continues by giving a history of preaching from Adam to St. Paul, concluding with these biblical questions: "How can they beleeve of whom they have not heard? and how can they heare without a Preacher?"[56] Bernard thus expresses the popular Puritan notion that preaching was always and still is the first priority of the ministry because by it God saves "all that shall be saved." William Ames emphatically declares the same of the ministry: that "the preaching of the word is of utmost importance, and so it has always been of continuous use in the church."[57] For the Puritan the Word of God was all important because hearing the word was the avenue to conversion and salvation. [58] In contrast, in "The Parson preaching" (as we have noted in chapter 1 and discuss further below), Herbert makes no specific mention of conversion or salvation, but instead focuses on the "art" of preaching (232:31) and sermon delivery.

Because of the sermon's importance to them, it is not surprising to find that the Puritan writers characteristically devote a great deal of attention to sermon preparation. Godly scholarship takes on a high priority to the Puritan manual writers. While Puritan preachers would refrain from showing their research in the pulpit, "their ideal," Perry Miller explains, "did demand discipline and much care for formal qualities." Miller continues: "The manuals called for simplicity, but did not believe that a minister should 'come into the place rawly and rudely, without serious meditation and preparation'; they declared that the 'sudden conceits of the minde, not digested, must needs be rawly delivered, and often little to the purpose.'"[59] Miller quotes John Eliot (whom he calls "conspicuous even among the pious of his generation for the simplicity of his spirit") as saying that he "lik'd no Preaching, but what had been WELL STUDIED for," and he quotes Cotton Mather as saying proudly of John Cotton that his "composures all smelt of the Lamp."[60] Richard Bernard, in his letter to his readers, warns that "zeale not according to knowledge breedeth but dissention,"[61] and he devotes eight full pages to listing the sources a preacher must master in order to write a proper sermon.[62] He includes books of grammar, languages, rhetoric, philosophy, economics, ethics, politics, geography, cosmography, history, books of "Trees, Herbes, Beasts, of Husbandrie . . . Waights and Measures," and of course books of divinity. Works one must have on hand are "First, the Bible, the booke of God in English, Latin, Greeke and Hebrue"; one must also have dictionaries, concordances, analytical expositions, annotations, a catechism, a commonplace book, commentaries ("of Orthodox writers"), ecclesiastical histories, the acts and canons of ancient counsels, the *Book of Martyrs*, and so on.

Bernard explains the use for such learning: "The diversitie of knowledge in severall things which a man brings with him to the reading of the Scripture, are as many candles to give light to see into his text," and he continues saying that his purposes in thus cataloguing these sources are "to shew [it is a] brain-sicke opinion to denie the use of Arts to the Scripture, and to stirre us up to the diligent study of these things . . . and [to recommend] that such as have children and would preferre them to the Ministrie should endevour to traine them up in all kinde of learning."[63]

Bernard seems thus to disprove thoroughly the notion that the Puritan was a man of one book. But lest we misunderstand the place of humane learning, Bernard concludes: "lastly, a Minister besides all these helpes, must have to rule and direct him in these subordinate meanes, the holie spirit of God, the onely true interpretour of the Scriptures."[64]

William Perkins likewise expresses the need for the liberal arts in the ministry. He places them at the top of the prerequisites for the vocation: "First, if every true Minister must bee Gods Interpreter to the people, and the peoples to God, then hence we learne that every one, who either is or intends to be a minister, must have that tongue of the learned."[65] Perkins then elucidates: "But to be able to speake with this tongue is, first TO BE FURNISHED WITH HUMANE LEARNING. Secondly, WITH DIVINE KNOWLEDGE."[66] Also like Bernard, Perkins carefully enunciates the incompleteness of uninspired scholarship: "Indeede we bee MANS INTERPRETER by humane teaching, and may interpret the Scriptures, truely and soundly, as a humane booke or storie for the increase of knowledge, but the

DIVINE AND SPIRITUALL INTERPRETATION, which shall perce the heart, and astonish the soule of man, must bee taught by the inward teaching of the holy Ghost."[67] Perkins thus places a high premium on human knowledge, but he also insists upon the minister's reliance on the Holy Spirit to "perce the heart and astonish the soule" of men. But Perkins will not rest until he has made his position completely clear. Thus he distinguishes the Puritan reliance on the Holy Spirit from that of the more radical Protestants: "Let no man thinke I heere give the least allowance to Anabaptisticall fancies, and revelations which are nothing . . . for they contemne both humane learning, and the study of the Scripture, and trust wholy to revelations of the spirit . . . I teach this, that a Minister . . . after all his owne study, meditation, conference, Commentaries, & after all humane helps, hee must pray with David, 'Open thou mine eyes, that I may see the wonders of thy law.' The discerning of those wonders requires a spirituall illumination and the opening of them requires the tongue of the learned."[68] Spiritual illumination and the tongue of the learned used in the service of preaching toward conversion—such were the priorities for the ministry given in most seventeenth-century English ministerial handbooks, though not in George Herbert's *The Country Parson.*

As we have already noted, Herbert does not emphasize conversion, nor does he treat preaching as the single most important task of the ministry. J. Sears McGee argues that Anglicans "were frequently skeptical about the value of what Puritans insisted was the staff of spiritual life, the sermon."[69] Anglicans naturally found fault with the sermon as the Puritans' chief pride and weapon against the established church. This may partially account for Herbert's reluctance to write a panegyric on the sermon as his fellow authors so often do. Perhaps, too, it accounts for the surprising difference of emphasis between the way all other manual authors treat sermon writing and the way Herbert treats it in "The Parson preaching."[70] But McGee's rubric distinguishing Anglican and Puritan on the basis of their devotion to First or Second Table duties unfortunately cannot extend an explanation to Herbert's unusual preference for experience over books in sermon preparation.[71] This predilection places Herbert in quite a contrast with the other manual authors. Bernard and

Perkins, and most other authors devote significant portions of their treatises to recommending texts, insisting on the need for humane learning, or showing how the minister is to use his sources and knowledge to expostulate the scriptures.

After reading these treatises, the reader of *The Country Parson* might feel in Herbert's work an uneasy suggestion of anti-intellectualism. While Richard Bernard, for example, insists "a Minister must have a good librarie"[72] and provides lists of books to fill it, George Herbert insists, "The Country Parson's Library is a holy life" (278:11). Herbert does not blatantly deny the usefulness of scholarly sources, nor does he rely exclusively on the inner movements of the Holy Spirit as an Anabaptist might. But neither "the tongue of the learned" nor "spiritual illumination" receives the honor with Herbert that they do with most other manualists. "Spiritual illumination" may perhaps be an aid to sermon writing more claimed by Puritans than other Anglicans, but surely "the tongue of the learned" would be recommended by High and Low Churchmen alike. It seems that Herbert's emphasis on experience cannot be explained by any desire to provide a balance or cut a middle path between Anglo-Catholic and Puritan trends. We shall therefore have to leave this subject for a later discussion, simply noting at this point that *The Country Parson*'s preference for experience over scholarly sources provides a remarkable contrast with other works of its kind.[73]

One final area of the philosophy of ministry, then, yet needs to be examined—what Herbert and his colleagues write about the use of "appearances." While it is not uncommon for clerical handbooks to give some advice on the parson's voice and gestures in the pulpit, the degree and kind of advice *The Country Parson* gives sets it off from other books of its genre. Herbert's chapters 6 and 7, "The Parson praying" and "The Parson preaching" pay a great deal of attention to the outward appearances of these tasks. Herbert's stress is undoubtedly upon the forms of prayer and preaching, though he does not altogether ignore the inner realities accompanying such forms. Regarding prayer, for example, Herbert begins by describing the appropriate gestures, not denying that they are related to the parson's own feelings, but placing his focus on their effects: "The Countrey Parson, when he is to read divine services, composeth himselfe to all possible reverence; lifting up his heart and hands, and eyes, and using all other gestures which may expresse a hearty, and unfeyned devotion . . . knowing that no Sermon moves [his people] so much to reverence, which they forget againe, when they come to pray, as a devout behaviour in the very act of praying. Accordingly his voyce is humble, his words treatable, and slow; yet not so slow neither, as to let the fervency of the supplicant hang and dy between speaking, but with a grave livelinesse, between fear and zeal, pausing yet pressing, he performes his duty" (231:1–20).

While other authors urge, "Pay attention to your own heart and your performance will take care of itself," Herbert's advice seems to be, "Pay attention to your performance and the hearts of your auditors will be moved."[74] Herbert mentions that the parson is himself "truly touched and amazed with the Majesty of God" (231:5), but this passing reference to the parson's heart reflects sentiments far removed from those of other authors. Gilbert Burnet explains: "a deep sense of the things prayed for, a true recollection and attention of spirit, and a holy earnestness of soul, will give a composure to the looks, and a weight to the pronunciation."[75] For most authors, appropriate gestures are a result of cultivated, heartfelt convictions. But with Herbert the gestures, not the feelings, must be cultivated. In the passage above Herbert tells his readers how to "perform" their prayers. Alternatively Burnet writes: "[The minister] must bring his mind to an inward and feeling sense of those things that are prayed for in our offices: that will make him pronounce them with an equal measure of gravity and affection . . . I do not love the theatrical way of the church of Rome, in which it is a great study, and a long practice, to learn in every one of their offices how they ought to compose their looks, gesture and voice."[76]

Like Burnet, Richard Baxter believes that true fervency begins in the heart, and he is critical of those whose fervency is a performance: "I should think it very necessary that, both before and in the work, we take special pains with our own hearts . . . An affected, hypocritical fervency will not hold out long in duties of this kind. A pulpit . . . is the hypocritical minister's stage.[77]

Herbert explains that when the parson is to preach he "procures attention by all possible art," and he coaches his readers on how to speak and look in the pulpit (232–35). Other manualists alternatively insist that "a gracious sanctified heart [is] the tuner of the voice."[78] William Ames writes, "Speech and action should be completely spiritual, flowing from the very heart."[79] While Herbert relies on the parson's "busy cast of his eye" (233:1) to keep his auditors' attention, other authors depend upon the Holy Spirit within the minister: "The doing of all these things must have in it no show of human wisdom or mixture of carnal affections; it should manifest itself throughout as the demonstration of the Spirit. I Corinthians 1:17; and 2:1, 4, 13, Not with skill of speaking . . . but . . . that which the Holy Spirit teaches."[80]

Richard Bernard writes: "Preaching should not be a labour of the lippes, or talke of the toong from a light imagination: but a serious meditation of the heart in grounded knowledge by much study and illumination of the spirit."[81] And William Perkins firmly states that pastors must "preach Gods word in THE EVIDENCE AND DEMONSTRATION OF THE SPIRIT OF GOD."[82] Herbert, on the other hand, never mentions the Holy Spirit in his discussions on sermon delivery.

Finally, while Herbert encourages the parson to appear holy, the other manualists urge their readers to an inner holiness. We have already noted the way in which Herbert encourages certain actions because they "shew very Holy" (234:36) or "appear exceeding reverend, and holy" (234:24) and the way in which he suggests certain words because they "carry great holiness in them" (234:1) or they have the "sign of holiness" (234:9). Alternatively, Richard Baxter warns against such "shews" of holiness: "woe to him that takes up with the fame of godliness, instead of godliness."[83] This is not to imply that Herbert himself was not a holy man, nor that he intentionally encouraged hypocrisy. The point here is that while most seventeenth-century handbooks for the ministry concentrated on cultivating the inner state or reality of piety, *The Country Parson* cultivates its appearance. Richard Baxter sums up the fears of all his fellow authors on this subject: "What though [the pastor] live civilly and preach plausibly, and maintain outwardly a profession of religion? He may be as fast in the devil's snares, by worldliness, pride, a secret distaste of diligent godliness, or by an unsound heart, that is not rooted in the faith, nor unreservedly devoted to Christ, as others are by drunkenness, uncleanness, and similar disgraceful sins . . . And though many of these men may seem excellent preachers, and may cry down sin as loudly as others, yet it is all but an affected fervency, and too commonly a mere useless bawling."[84]

Unlike Baxter, Herbert seemed to have no fears that the pastor would be "fast in the devil's snares"; he was concerned instead to teach him to "live civilly, and preach plausibly, and maintain outwardly a profession of religion." Thus we see Herbert undisturbed by the common suspicion of appearances in the ministry.

The Country Parson is something of an anomaly, then, among seventeenth century clerical handbooks. While showing a liking for Puritan trends in sermon preparation and the plain style, Herbert stands apart from his Puritan brethren in his seeming lack of interest in the salvation or sanctification of the minister, his lack of fervor about conversion (the minister's or the people's), his focus on good works rather than faith, his stress on sermon delivery over the content of a sermon, and his emphasis on the appearances or performances of holiness rather than on inner holiness itself. With no apologies, Herbert fashions his country parson using values and sensibilities from various traditions within the church. *The Country Parson* may be Herbert's answer to popular works like William Perkins's *Of the Calling of the Ministrie* and Richard Bernard's *The Faithfull Shepheard*, his attempt to counterbalance a genre dominated by Puritan voices. Herbert raises a mediating voice in a time when polarization was quickly on the increase, calling for a "middle way between superstition and slovenlinesse."

Yet not all of Herbert's remarkable choices in *The Country Parson* seem to be entirely motivated by religious or political impulses. Our next chapter will explore a possible literary source for Herbert's inspiration: the Renaissance courtesy book.

3
The Country Parson and Courtesy

In thy discourse, if thou desire to please,
All such is courteous, usefull, new, or wittie.
Usefulnesse comes by labour, wit by ease;
Courtesie grows in court; news in the citie.
Get a good stock of these, then draw the card
That suites him best, of whom thy speech is heard.
—George Herbert
"The Church Porch"

ON THE TITLE PAGE OF *OF THE CALLING OF THE MINISTERIE* ONE reads: "Delivered Publickly in the Universitie of Cambridge by Master Perkins. Taken then from his mouth, and now diligently perused and published."[1] The advertisement to John Jackson's *The Worthy Church-man* acknowledges a similar homiletic origin: "first glossed and scholyed on in a Synod–Sermon; and after enlarged by way of discourse."[2] *The Reformed Pastor,* too, although never actually preached because of Baxter's ill health, was composed specifically as an oral address.[3] Indeed, nearly every ministerial handbook published in the seventeenth century gives evidence of having been conceived as a sermon, and those manuals that do not explicitly acknowledge such beginnings display unmistakable characteristics of a sermon. All start with a scripture text; most take their structure from explicating a text part-by-part.[4] The author often addresses the readers as if they were physically present;[5] and most manuals have the oratorical markings of an easily discernible order and central point, repetition, and emphatic oral cadences.[6]

The Country Parson, however, shares none of these homiletic earmarks. In its preface, "The Authour to the Reader," Herbert expresses that he means to "*set down* the Form and Character of a true Pastour," and he specifically calls his work a "Book" (224:15). He gives no scripture text and employs no recognizable sermon structures or techniques. This work would, in fact, make a very poor sermon. Rather than a focused argument in the explication/application style, *The Country Parson* is a series of twenty-seven short, casually linked, self-contained discourses reflecting on the pastor's life in a familiar, and even intimate, tone. There is little urgency here, no public voice, and no obviously apparent order or thesis. Unlike most other pastoral handbooks, *The Country Parson* is neither derived from nor is it fashioned in the shape of a sermon.[7]

In chapter 1 we studied Herbert's concentration on the outer man or the "life" of the country parson, as opposed to the inner man and his doctrine or faith. Chapter 2, in contrasting Herbert with other writers of clerical manuals, concluded that Herbert's uniqueness stems in part from his desire to provide an Anglican contribution to a largely Puritan genre and to urge a "middle way between superstition, and slovenlinesse." This chapter continues the argument, asserting that Herbert crafted *The Country Parson* in such a way as to underscore his emphasis on outer appearances. Herbert's choice of a secular literary model for his manual instead of the more typical religious homiletic model demonstrates a particular care for form, which many Puritan authors commonly ignored in their utilitarian transposing of sermon into manual.[8] In both message and execution, *The Country Parson* is Herbert's attempt to shake off "slovenlinesse" in the ministry and to do things "decently" (246:24–27).

Instead of the sermon, the model *The Country Parson* follows is the popular Renaissance courtesy book. The courtesy book was peculiarly suited to provide a vehicle for Herbert's ideas on the British ministry. *The Country Parson* manifests striking resemblances to the courtesy manual in its aristocratic tone or temper, courtly diction, and courtesy topics, themes, and techniques.

That Herbert used courtesy themes and strategies has been noted before—especially in regard to his poetry.[9] Michael Schoenfeldt in *Prayer and Power: George Herbert and Renaissance Courtship* sums up Herbert's use of courtly themes this way: "Herbert writes like one whose business is most with God precisely because he uses the language of social exchange in his spiritual encounters with God. His heart-work and heaven-work are expressed in the idiom of court-work."[10] In examining courtesy themes, language, and strategies in Herbert's poetry, Schoenfeldt illuminates Herbert's poetic achievement. Viewing *The Country Parson* in light of the courtesy tradition will prove just as fruitful as the studies of Herbert's poetry in that light have been.

An acute awareness of social distinctions constitutes one element in Herbert's writing that sets him apart from the other manual authors and is highly suggestive of the courtesy genre. The modern reader who knows the often self-effacing poet of *The Temple* may be surprised by the persistently aristocratic tone of *The Country Parson.* Here Herbert shows himself to be highly sensitive to class distinctions. Herbert suggests, for example, that the parson should occasionally invite the poor to his table, "whom he sometimes purposely takes home with him, setting them by him, and carving for them." It is hard to mistake Herbert's class consciousness when he explains that the parson condescends to such hospitality "for his own humility" (243:9–12). Henry Peacham's class consciousness is similarly expressed in this recommendation for his "compleat gentleman": "[Not] that I would deny a Prince or Gentleman the benefit of discourse and converse with the meanest: for Majesty and Greatnesse cannot always stand so bent, but it must have remission and relaxation sometime to descend from court to cottage, which cannot choose but give [the court] the better taste and rellish."[11]

This condescending tone is not surprising in a courtesy book, but it strikes an unusual cord in a clerical manual. Similarly, in visitation, Herbert suggests that the parson "neither disdaineth . . . to enter into the poorest Cottage, though he even creep into it, and though it smell never [*sic*] so lothsomly." Such a task is obviously offensive to Herbert's sensibilities. Part of the virtue in making the visit is the opportunity for humility that it affords: Herbert writes of the pastor in such a situation, "in regard of himselfe, it is . . . humiliation" (249:4–9).

Underscoring his awareness of social hierarchy, Herbert entitles a chapter on the parson's participation in local ceremonies as "The Parson's Condescending" (283–84). Despite the genuine concern Herbert expresses toward his people, there is no mistaking his aristocratic attitudes. His generalizations about his working-class parishioners are less than flattering; for example, about their daily behavior he writes: "Country people are full of . . . petty injustices, being cunning to make use of another, and spare themselves" (265:33–35). He attributes an unspiritual disposition to their close ties to nature: "considering the great aptnesse Countrey people have to think that all things come by a kind of naturall course . . . that if they sow and soyle their grounds, they must have corn" (270:24–26).

Very much in the spirit of courtesy authors, Herbert recommends differing treatment for the "plaine countryman" and the man of "higher quality" (248:17–18). He is convinced of the typical working man's mental and even spiritual inferiority. He suggests, for instance, that the parson make use of material gifts when his "plaine countrymen" are good and that he withhold such things when they are not because these material incentives for sanctification are the only sort that the laborer understands: "Thus both in rewarding vertue, and in punishing vice, the Parson endeavoureth to be in Gods stead, knowing that Countrey people are drawne, or led by sense, more then faith, by present rewards, or punishments, more then by future" (254:29–33).[12] His description of rural parishioners in church is striking: "Sometimes [the preacher] tells them stories, and sayings of others according as his text invites him; for them also men heed, and remember better then exhortations; which though earnest, yet often dy with the Sermon, especially with Countrey people; which are thick, and heavy and hard to raise to a poynt of zeal, and fervency, and need a mountaine of fire to kindle them; but stories and sayings they will well remember." (233:11–18).

This unflattering picture of the common man—"thick, heavy, and hard to raise to a poynt of zeal"—is persistent in *The Country Parson.*

The Country Parson exudes an unmistakable aristocratic temper. Herbert's work stands out in this regard. Most of the period's other guides-to-godliness and clerical manuals have instead a decidedly democratic and middle-class spirit.[13] Although a country parson, Herbert retains a strongly upper-class, urbane awareness of social lines, and he has difficulty hiding this attitude for all that he might believe that God is "no respecter of persons."

A partial explanation of Herbert's uniqueness, of course, is social: nearly all of Herbert's fellow manual authors were middle-class Puritans while Herbert was a blue-blooded Anglican. Herbert's family was among the most aristocratic in England at the time. As a young man, he entertained high hopes in the court of King James where the courtesy book, a manual for self-improvement specifically designed for the novice at court, was very popular among aspiring young courtiers. *The Country Parson* certainly reflects the class conscious tone of works belonging to that genre. Herbert's sometimes pitying, sometimes condescending, aristocratic attitude toward the lower class closely resembles the attitude taken traditionally by courtesy authors.

Courtesy books were a product of class consciousness and cultivated it as well. In her work on the courtesy book, *The Doctrine of the English Gentleman in the Sixteenth Century,* Ruth Kelso explains how very far the heart of the courtesy tradition was from the democratic spirit of the later Puritan clerical manuals: "courtesy as a gentlemanly virtue was fundamentally a preserver of society, helping to keep the lines between classes that the aristocratic ideal created."[14] As an aristocrat himself, it is not so surprising that Herbert would write like one. By writing like a courtesy author and emphasizing class distinctions, Herbert tacitly supports the social hierarchy which more extreme Protestants like the Quakers and Levelers abhorred. Herbert can assume superiority over his parishioners because he as a parson himself is a man under authority. He explains, for example, that the country parson must use the church catechism "for obedience to Authority" (255:17), and he instructs the country parson to honor his superiors: "[the parson] carryes himself very respectively, as to all the Fathers of the Church, so especially to his Diocesan, honouring him in both word, and behaviour, and resorting unto him in any difficulty, either in his studies or in his Parish" (253:5–9). Herbert's conservative spirit, thus strongly supporting the social and religious hierarchy, is not typical among the more democratic-sounding voices of contemporary clerical manuals.

If *The Country Parson* resembles a courtesy book in its persistent awareness (and support) of social distinctions, its metaphors also are highly suggestive of courtly titles and relationships. Of all of the metaphorical descriptions of the spiritual life, Herbert overwhelmingly prefers those which make a comparison between the earthly, civil powers and the heavenly. Here, for instance, he describes the fawning behavior of some chaplains who show a preference for the temporal court over the eternal: "They who do . . . thus, while they remember their earthly Lord, do much forget their heavenly" (226:31–33). In describing the parson's obligation to teach his children spiritual truths, he compares one commonwealth with the other: "His children he first makes Christians, and then Commonwealths–men; the one he owes to his heavenly Countrey, the other to his earthly, having no title to either, except he do good to both" (239:19–23). Herbert is not unique in his analogies of the Divinity to "King," "Majesty," and "Judge" (e.g., 234:31; 235:23; 236:5; 233:21). Nevertheless, his consistent preference for such appositives for God as "the Great Governour of all things" (281:10) enhances the courtly ambiance of his manual.

Most suggestive of courtesy language is the vocabulary Herbert uses to describe the parson himself. If God is the King of the spiritual court, the country parson is a civil servant. Herbert defines the parson in this way in his opening chapter, "Of a Pastor." Here he explains, "A Pastor is the Deputy of Christ" and God's "Vicegerent" (225:1, 17). As a noble or gentleman is the king's representative to the shire, "The Countrey Parson is in Gods stead to his Parish" (254:8). Herbert describes the parson sometimes in martial terms, as if he were God's courtly knight protecting the countryside. Chapter 18 he calls "The Parson in Sentinel" and explains that "The Countrey Parson, where ever he is, keeps Gods watch; that is there is nothing spoken, or done in the Company where he is, but comes under his Test and censure" (252:1–3). Although here Herbert describes the congregation in the conventional term as sheep, again the parson is described more like an active knight than a contemplative cleric:

"The Countrey Parson at spare times from action, stand[s] on a hill, and considers his Flock." (264:3–4). Herbert conceives of the spiritual life as a battle in which the parson–knight must pick up his arms and fight for his king: "This is to be on Gods side, and be true to his party" (252:14–15).

In addition to this chivalric language, Herbert also describes the parson in terms that associate him with the aristocracy and the privileges and obligations of that class. In his descriptions of the parson's charity, for example, he suggests not the New Testament pattern for giving found in the story of the widow's mite, but the noblesse oblige of the Renaissance aristocracy. He majestically calls his giving "times of opening his hand" (245:6) and discusses this charity in a chapter he significantly entitles "The Parson's Courtesie" (chapter 11). Herbert explains, "The Country Parson owing a debt of Charity to the poor, and of Courtesie to his other parishioners, he so distinguisheth, that he keeps his money for the poor, and his table for those that are above alms" (243:6–9). The parson owes this "debt of Charity," not because his Master has bid him to "go and sell all he has and give to the poor," but because (as all courtesy books make clear) one must not "pinch, and scrape, and squeeze blood undecently to the station wherein God hath placed [one]" (265:17–18). Herbert extends this metaphor of noblesse oblige even to the parson's words, explaining, "these exhortations he cals his privy purse, even as Princes have theirs" (236:16–18). Far more than the typical metaphors of shepherd, interpreter, messenger, or ploughman appearing in most ministerial handbooks, Herbert prefers for the parson the courtly metaphor of God's civil servant.

In addition to its aristocratic temper and courtly language, *The Country Parson* shows an affinity to the courtesy genre in its choice of topics. Although Herbert's treatment of these subjects is more unmistakably Christian than is that by the typical secular courtesy author, it is significant that Herbert discusses such issues at all. In the tradition of *The Courtier, The Galateo,* and *Civile Conversation, The Country Parson* gives advice on eating (e.g., 241:15–19; 266:5–67:26), complementing and speech (252:4–12; 286:19–25; 285–288), apparel (228:8–13; 265:15), the use of wealth (265:5–266:5, 274:28–275:5), riding and arms (252:

24–29; 277:14–18), idleness (274:9), travel (278:3–10), and the training of noblemen's sons (276–78). Other authors of clerical manuals avoid such subjects altogether, preferring instead to focus on more distinctly spiritual matters.

Most like a courtesy book in subject matter is the long chapter 32, "The Parson's Surveys" (274–278). When the parson "surveys" England he finds "the great and nationall sin" of the land to be "idlenesse" (274:8–9). Herbert apparently agrees with Stefano Guazzo that: "there is nothing more dangerous than an idle young man."[15] Idleness is the same sin which Richard Brathwaite loudly condemned in his courtesy book, *The English Gentleman,*[16] published two years before Herbert wrote *The Country Parson.* Like Brathwaite, Herbert urges "to every body the necessity of a vocation" (274:17–18). More like the English courtesy authors than the continental on this point, Herbert condemns the lounging life of the gallant and gives instructions to either "have a Calling, or prepare for it" (275:11).[17] Herbert's manual is similar to a courtesy book in its specific instructions to the upper class against idleness. To the idle nobleman he suggests improvement of his grounds—"by drowning, or draining, or stocking, or fencing" (275:24–25)—or civil service (275:36–276:16). To those preparing for a calling, heirs and younger brothers, he also gives specific advice. With heirs he discusses "Sessions and Sizes," the court, travel, the Parliament, horsemanship, and military service. With younger brothers Herbert advises on dressing, complimenting, visiting, and sporting, the law, mathematics, and travel (277:1–278:10).[18]

Such subjects are rarely if ever discussed by other writers of clerical handbooks; however, they are the standard fare of contemporary works of courtesy, and Herbert's topics read like their tables of contents. Richard Cleland's *Institution of a Young Noble Man,* for example, includes similar discussions on "Mathematickes," "the Lawes," "Of a Noblemans duty towards the King," "Of his behauiour at Court," "How a Noble man should speake," "Of his diet in eating and drinking," "Of his Apparel," "Of Riding, Shooting . . . and handling of Armes," and "Of Trauelling." Henry Peacham's *The Compleat Gentleman* also provides chapters on these typical courtesy themes: "Of Geometry," "Of reputation and carriage," "Of Trauile," and "Of Warre." Like any courtesy author, Herbert offers advice to young noblemen to help suit them for their future places among the country's elite.

Herbert's description of the parson's life reflects another significant motif in *The Country Parson.* Herbert writes: "The Country Parson is exceeding exact in his Life, being holy, just, prudent, temperate, bold, grave in all his wayes" (227:1–3). This language is significant and unusual for a pastoral guide. Herbert is here describing not the typical minister of the clerical manual, but the courtly gentleman of the courtesy book. Like all courtesy authors, Herbert builds his definition of the perfect gentleman on the Aristotelian moral virtues of justice, prudence, temperance, and fortitude.[19] While no two lists of virtues are identical, all courtesy authors build upon this frame. Castiglione in The *Courtier,* for instance, lists "continence, fortitude, justice, and temperance" as the most primary virtues of courtier and prince.[20] The man of honor must possess wisdom, justice, fortitude, and temperance according to Guazzo.[21] Thomas Elyot devotes an entire third of *The Book Named the Governor* to analyzing and recommending justice, fortitude, temperance, and prudence.[22] Peacham describes fortitude, justice, magnificence (liberality), and eloquence with classical examples as incentives to young noblemen to read and follow his book.[23] And Spenser's *Faerie Queene,* a courtesy book on the grandest scale, is organized around holiness, temperance, chastity, friendship, justice, and courtesy. Despite the variations in detail, by common consent the virtues of justice, prudence, courtesy, liberality, temperance, and fortitude were considered the most important for the gentleman.[24] The Christian theological virtues of faith, hope, and charity were given surprisingly little attention in comparison.

Ruth Kelso suggests why the classical virtues were chosen over the Christian ones as a moral foundation for the genre: "The Christian ideal is built upon humility, abasement before God and before man, denial of self for the sake of others; the aristocratic ideal assumes inherent inequalities between men and works for the perfection of a few at the expense of the many. For such an ideal the Aristotelian code is an admirable guide, exalting as it does the individual, expanding his powers and developing a proud consciousness of superiority."[25] Indeed, how could the theological virtues of faith, hope, and love, or the fruits of the Spirit—love, joy, peace, patience, kindness, goodness, gentleness, and self control (Galatians 5:22)—serve as practical guides for a genre dedicated to worldly advancement?

To be sure, nearly all courtesy authors, both English and continental, would consider themselves Christian, but this did not dampen their enthusiasm for the classical ideal. Rather than acknowledging any possible inconsistency between religion and ethic, these authors often added to the classical virtues Christian ones (as Spenser and Herbert add holiness to their lists) with no apparent consciousness that inconsistencies might exist.[26] If courtesy authors saw the classical virtues as compatible with or preparatory to the Christian virtues, they neglected to explain such a relationship. Religious truths were never deliberately undermined, but they were passed over nonetheless when these authors chose the moral foundation for their works: "It was freely admitted that anything incompatible with religion must be rejected, but the reader was generally left to judge for himself what was compatible, and at the best he was presented with a code of ethics that was pagan in ground and frame, and in large measure in the spirit also."[27]

While the seventeenth-century courtesy book followed a long tradition that was "pagan in the ground and frame," the typical clerical manual derived its ethic and inspiration almost exclusively from the Bible. Herbert, however, deviates from this pattern, preferring to describe his parson primarily by the courtly virtues rather than the biblical ones of faith, hope, and charity.[28] Once again Herbert seeks a balance in scales usually tipped rather to the Puritan side.

Other authors writing advice to clergy overwhelmingly wrote in the Puritan style—prodigiously quoting the Bible and rarely making classical references. This was the rule in all nonconformist literature. Although Puritan divines insisted that seminarians and pastors study the classics along with many other disciplines, they saw little value in citing classical references to the public.[29] This view contributed inadvertently to a growing popular opinion that any spiritual Christian could preach the Bible. William Haller notes: "The learned [Puritan] preachers had practiced the art of concealing art in the pulpit and had taught the doctrine of the gift or calling to such effect that many who were not learned but felt inspired knew exactly how the spirit within them might be expected to express itself. What they meant was that men had equal rights to seek truth in scripture and, no matter how poor or ignorant, to think and speak for themselves upon any subject, such as the salvation of their souls, which closely concerned them."[30] Extreme pamphlets appeared insisting that humane learning was in fact handicap to the soul. Samual How, a cobbler, wrote *The Sufficiencie of the Spirits Teaching without human learning: or a Treatise tending to prove humane Learning to be no help to the spirituall understanding of the Word of God*. And John Spencer, a coachman, wrote *A Short Treatise concerning the lawfullnesse of every mans exercising his gift as God shall call him thereunto*. Such broadsides argued that a spirit–filled man, like the young, unlearned Christ in the Temple among the scribes, knows better than all the doctors of the universities.[31]

Given this antihumanistic climate, Herbert's classical debts are striking. His surprisingly "classical" parson sets his work apart from the other pastoral manuals. At one point he even argues that St. Luke, Tertullian, and Chrysostom are at least as trustworthy as Tully, Virgil, and Livy (282:21–23). This high regard for the classical/courtly virtues may provide a partial explanation for yet another way in which *The Country Parson* resembles a courtesy book: a shared concern with appearances.

We have already discovered the large and unusual place given to appearances in general in *The Country Parson.*[32] Although Herbert does not specifically name them in his list of the parson's virtues, liberality and courtesy play significant roles in the life of Herbert's parson. In methodology and technique, though not in ultimate purpose, Herbert uses the outward manifestations of liberality and courtesy after the manner of courtesy authors.[33]

The classical virtue of liberality is radically different from the Christian ideal of generosity. The Christian ideal is based upon obedience, compassion, and anonymity; that is, obedience to God, compassion toward the needy, and anonymity regarding one's own giving ("let not your left hand know what your right hand is doing"—Matthew 6:3). Liberality, on the other hand, was originally defined by Aristotle simply as the mean between avarice and extravagance and came to be valued among the courtesy authors more for its temporal benefits than its spiritual ones. Jeronimo Osorius in *Civile Nobilitie* (1542) writes of liberality: "Neyther truly is there any vertue which doth more become a noble minde, or setteth forthe more a worthy wight, either that winneth more praise & commendation, and getteth more goodwill, love, and reverence; without which no man may maytayn his owne estate or attayne to live in any worshipful calling."[34] Liberality, Osorius explains, cultivates goodwill, love, and reverence. Rather than obedience to God, the chief impetus to liberality is utilitarian. One gives, not so much from compassion for suffering as from a desire for praise and commendation. Anonymity, of course, would defeat the purposes of liberality—engendering respect and serviceableness. Castiglione, for instance, recommends that the noble give according to merit so that he may be better loved by his constituents: "[The Courtier] ought to love those close to him according to their rank, maintaining with all men a strict equality in certain things such as justice and liberty; and in certain other things, a reasonable inequality, such as being generous, in rewarding, in distributing honors and dignities according to the differences in their merits, which ought always to be surpassed by their rewards and not the other way around; *and in this way he would be not only loved but almost adored by his subjects.*"[35]

Machiavelli's singular courtesy book, *The Prince,* most clearly demonstrates the self-seeking nature of liberality: "A prince ought also to show himself an admirer of talent, giving recognition to men of ability and honoring those who excel in a particular art. The prince should bestow prizes on the men . . . and anyone else who takes the pains to enrich the city or state in some special way. The prince who wants to keep his minister obedient should think of his welfare, honor him, enrich him, load him with honors and offices. *Thus the minister will not be able to stand without the prince.*"[36]

In brief Stefano Guazzo explains, "riches well bestowed, are a great ornament, and setting forth to a gentleman."[37]

Herbert's descriptions of the parson's giving have something of this utilitarian flavor. The parson gives to relieve the poor, but also to inspire in them a love and respect for himself. Herbert writes: "he gives [the poor] somewhat; and opens not only his mouth, but his purse to their relief, that so they go on more cheerfully in their vocation, *and himself be ever the more welcome to them*" (248:10–13, my italics). This spirit of liberality is far from the world–abandoning spirit of selling all one has to follow Christ. Instead, for the courtesy author, liberality rather is a very calculated giving meant to encourage the receiver on to appropriate grateful behavior. Ruth Kelso writes: "Promiscuous giving was no part of true liberality; for two reasons: such giving might do harm to the recipient and no good to the giver; and it was incompatible with the virtue of prudence which the gentleman was preeminently expected to show. Rewards judiciously bestowed would act as spurs to further effort on the part of the recipient and also others who would be led to hope for similar reward."[38]

Herbert clearly believes in the necessity of such selective generosity. "The Parson's Charity" makes plain both the harm of "promiscuous" giving and the benefits of "rewards judiciously bestowed": "But [the parson] gives no set pension to any; for this in time will lose the name and effect of Charity with the poor people. . . but the Parson having a double aime, and making a hook of his Charity, causeth them still to depend on him; and so by continuall and fresh bounties, unexpected to them, but resolved to himself, hee wins them to praise God more, to live more religiously, and to take more paines in their vocation. . . yet in all his Charity, he distinguisheth, giving them most, who live best, and take most paines, and are most charged: So is his charity in effect a Sermon" (244:25–245:17).

Herbert's purpose is to win his people "to praise God more." But in "making a hook of his Charity," Herbert retains the aristocratic goal of liberality, which is causing "them to still depend on him." His "double aime" is similar to that of all liberal gentlemen, that is, to give, both for the good of the people and the good of one's own position. His method is identical to that recommended by courtesy manuals; his gifts are meant as "spurs to further effort on the part of the recipient." The parson "distinguisheth, giving them most, who live best, and take most paines, and are most charged."

By practicing liberality, "The donor would be forwarding not only the welfare of the individual but that of the whole commonwealth, and at the same time would be creating in men's hearts love and reverence for himself, the true foundation of obedience."[39] Herbert recommends giving both to make the parson "ever the more welcome" to his people (248:10–13) and for the improvement of his parish, and he continually emphasizes the utilitarian purposes of giving. Here he describes how one might use giving to improve his parish: "The Countrey Parson is in Gods stead to his Parish, and dischargeth God what he can of his promises. *Wherefore there is nothing done either wel or ill, whereof he is not the rewarder, or punisher.* If he chance to finde any reading in anothers Bible, he provides him one of his own. If he finde another giving a poor man a penny, he gives him a tester for it, if the giver be fit to receive it; or if he be of a condition above such gifts, he sends him a good book, or easeth him in his Tithes, telling him when he hath forgotten it, This I do because at such, and such a time you were charitable. This is in some sort a discharging of God; as concerning this life, who hath promised that *Godlinesse shall be gainfull"* (254:8–20, my italics).

Herbert believes in such rewards in part because of his aristocratic views of the social disparities within his congregation. Here, for example, he expresses a particularly low view of his country parishioners' spirituality: "Thus both in rewarding vertue, and in punishing vice, the Parson endeavoureth to be in Gods stead, knowing that Countrey people are drawne, or led by sense, more then by faith, by present rewards or punishments, more then by future" (254:29–33). Like most courtesy authors, it would seem that Herbert here agrees with Machiavelli: liberality works because "Men are much more attracted by immediate than by remote events; when they find things going well in the here and now, they are pleased, and think of nothing else."[40] Herbert admits that such tactics are perhaps not the best, but he employs them because they work: "So the Countrey Parson . . . sets up as many encouragements to goodnesse as he can, both in honour, and profit, and fame; that he may, if not the best way, yet any way, make his Parish good" (244:1–5).

The gentleman's liberality toward himself constitutes an aspect of liberality that is also part of Herbert's sensibility. The courtly gentleman was expected to display his ability to be generous first by a generosity toward himself. Fine clothes, good food, and other worldly amenities argue against a small, mean spirit and show one to be in a position to share such goods with others.

Castiglione recommends that the nobleman surround himself with splendid things and events to show himself generous and above petty cares: "[The Prince] ought to be very generous and splendid . . . he ought to offer magnificent banquets, festivals, games, public shows; and have a great many fine horses for use in war and for pleasure in time of peace, falcons, dogs, and all the other things that pertain to the pleasures of great lords."[41] And Sir Thomas Elyot explains that the gentleman should avoid all appearances of stinginess by dressing in a way appropriate to his rank: "So is there apparel comely to every estate and degree . . . in a nobleman specially. For apparel simple or scanty reproveth him of avarice."[42]

Similarly, Herbert's definition of covetousness reflects this philosophy of liberality toward oneself prominent in courtesy material: "Whosever when a just occasion cals, either spends not at all, or not in some proportion to Gods blessing upon him, is covetous. The reason of the ground is manifest, because wealth is given to that end to supply our occasions. . . in brief, a poor man is an occasion . . . my Table is an occasion, my apparell is an occasion: if in all these, *and those more which concerne me,* I either do nothing, or pinch, and scrape, and squeeze blood undecently to the station wherein God hath placed me, I am Covetous" (265:5–19, my italics).

Herbert here elevates self-denial or stinginess toward oneself to a sin. Liberality dictates that the gentleman be appropriately generous toward himself. Herbert so far agrees with this principle to call its breach "covetousness." While Herbert's use of covetousness here may be in perfect keeping with courtesy sensibilities, it is strikingly different from that of other authors of religious manuals. Thomas Watson's exposition on the tenth commandment (in *A Body of Practical Divinity*) provides an example of the more common understanding of covetousness. He explains that covetousness "signifies an insatiable desire of getting the world," or "an inordinate love of the world."[43] Herbert defines covetousness as living below "the station wherein God hath placed me," and neglecting to give "thy need, thine honour, and thy friend his due." While Watson defines covetousness primarily as an inappropriate love for this world's goods, Herbert defines it as depriving oneself inappropriately of the same goods. Herbert calls neglecting one's table, apparel, and honor covetousness. Watson writes contrarily that covetousness "has many pleas and excuses for itself, more than any other sin; as providing for one's family."[44] Watson describes covetousness primarily as a sin of the heart and mind,[45] Herbert as a sin against one's body and appearance.

In his opening poem to *The Temple,* "The Church–Porch," Herbert expresses this peculiarly courtly definition of covetousness. He writes, "Be Thriftie, but not covetous: therefore give / Thy need, thine honour, and thy friend his due. / Never was scraper brave man" (12:151–53). As we read the first line of this stanza, it seems as if Herbert is recommending Christian charity: "Be thriftie, but not covetous: therefore give." The line stops here and so we momentarily feel that Herbert means for us to give selflessly and generally, according to need. But he does not. The command to give is qualified; give "thy need, thine honour, and thy friend his due." Giving to one's own need, honor, and friends is quite different from the ideal of Christian giving, but is entirely consonant with the classical concept of liberality extolled by the courtesy tradition. When Herbert defines covetousness as "pinching, and scraping, and squeezing blood undecently to the station wherein God hath placed me," and when he writes that one must be generous especially in those areas that concern oneself ("and *those more* which concerne me"), the similarity between Herbert's liberality and that of contemporary courtesy authors is unmistakable.

A further connection between Herbert and the courtesy tradition is suggested by the use of "courtesy" in *The Country Parson.* As with liberality, Herbert employs courtesy after the manner of courtesy book authors.

Although courtesy was sometimes Christianized, like liberality, justice, prudence, temperance, and fortitude, courtesy is fundamentally a secular virtue. It draws its inspiration not from the

Christian injunction to "do unto others as you would have them do unto you," but from a fundamental belief in the inequality of men. The golden rule of courtesy is not "do as you wish to be done by," but rather, "give each man his due," his due being determined by his place in the social hierarchy. Courtesy "is not the same thing for all men, but one thing for superiors, another for equals, and yet another for inferiors."[46] Thus, as Guazzo expressed it, the courtesy author instructs the young gentleman on "how to behave . . . towards others, *according to the difference of their estates*."[47] While courtesy can appear to be the flower of society in a book like Castiglione's *The Courtier*, where little mention is ever made of life outside of the courtly circle, in most courtesy manuals, the authors' references to other classes betrays the essentially utilitarian function of courtesy: to gain the favor of one's betters and (as with liberality) elicit reverence and gratitude of one's inferiors.

Whatever benefits courtesy might have on society as a whole, the Renaissance gentleman, for whom the courtesy book was written, was chiefly concerned with himself. And while the courtesy book may have truly helped beautify society, the other goals of the genre—preserving societal lines, prescribing behavior due each class and adorning the individual—are utilitarian in method and largely self-serving in aim. Here Lyly defines courtesy's meaning and purpose: "It is sober and descret behaviour, civil and gentle demeanor, *that in court winneth both credit and commoditie*."[48] Della Casa, in *The Galateo,* without apology explains that courtesy is a more useful virtue than justice, fortitude, and liberality because courtesy is more likely to advance its possessor:

> And albeit Liberalitie, or magnanimitie, of themselves beare a greater praise, then, to be a well taught or manored man: yet perchaunce, the courteous behaviour and entertainement with good maners and words, helpe no lesse, him that hath them: then the high minde and courage, advaunceth him in whome they be. But justice, fortitude, and the other greater, and more noble vertues, are seldome put in uze. And, if I could wel intend it, I could name you many, whoe, (being otherwise of litle account) have ben & be still, muche estemed & made of, for their cherefull & pleasaunt behaviour alone: which hath bin suche a

helpe & advauncement unto them, that they have gotten greate preferments, leaving farre behinde them, such men as have bin endowed with those other noble and better vertues spoken of before.[49]

Guazzo explains that courteous manners endear one to his superiors: "these worldly ceremonies purchase us the good will of our friendes and superiors." At the same time, courtesy ingratiates one to his inferiors: "[Gentlemen] ought to beholde their inferiours with a more gracious eye, and to use curtesie towards them . . . by meanes whereof, they get the good will of their worsers." Thus, Guazzo explains, the "worsers" are induced "to love [the gentleman], to honor him, and to doe him service."[50] Castiglione too describes courtesy as an expedient virtue. Here he recommends courteous behavior according to its relative serviceableness: "it seems to me that the right rule of conduct . . . consists in . . . discerning what the relative gain or loss is in things if done opportunely or done out of season.[51] By gain or loss, Castiglione refers to obtaining respect from inferiors and admiration from equals and superiors. In the opening lines of *The Courtier* Castiglione makes the utilitarian purpose of his courtesy book entirely clear: "Now you have asked me to write my opinion as to what form of Courtiership most befits a gentleman living at the courts of princes, by which he can have both the knowledge and the ability to serve them in every reasonable thing, *thereby winning favor from them and praise from others:* in short, what manner of man he must be who deserves the name of perfect Courtier."[52]

Herbert likewise recommends courtesy for its utility. As the courtesy book authors prescribe a certain kind of behavior to encourage respect and love from one's social inferiors, so Herbert instructs his parson to cultivate in his parishioners good will toward himself. Guazzo notes that "as there is nothing more hurtfull [for the gentleman] then to bee hated, so is there nothing more helpfull then to bee loved. Which no doubt is gotten with gentlenesse and curtesie."[53] Castiglione writes that he would have his courtier "loved and revered by everyone,"[54] and Machiavelli insists that the prince must keep "himself in popular favor."[55] Herbert similarly writes of the parson: "he endeavours that none shall despise him; especially in his own Parish" (268:17–18). To that end Herbert recommends courteous behavior. In "The Parson's Courtesie" Herbert explains that parishioners must occasionally be invited to the parson's home because, "countrey people are very observant of such things, and will not be perswaded, but being not invited, they are hated. Which perswasion the Parson by all means avoyds" (243:20–23). As with liberality, Herbert uses courtesy to gain the respect of his people. He recommends "a courteous carriage, & winning behaviour . . . doing kindnesses, but receiving none," because "this argues a height and eminency of mind, which is not easily despised" (268:22–26). Herbert's suggestion for using courtesy to win the love and to avoid the displeasure of one's inferiors is a common courtesy theme. Sir Thomas Elyot provides a typical example of this theme as he recommends affability to the gentleman: "Affability is of a wonderful efficacy or power in procuring love. And it is in sundry wise, but most properly, where a man is facile or easy to be spoken unto. It is also where a man speaketh courteously, with a sweet speech or countenance, wherewith the hearers (as it were with a delicate odour) be refreshed and allured to love him in whom is the most delectable quality."[56] Another Englishman, Henry Peacham concurs: "Affability and curtesie in Greatnesse, draweth our eyes like flowers in the Spring, to behold, and with admiration to love it wheresoever we find it."[57]

While the ultimate ends of the parson's courtesy are different from those of the courtier, Herbert's utilitarian use of courtesy is remarkably similar to that of the courtesy tradition. Herbert explains here, for example, how a parson is to use courtesy for spurring his parish on to good works and perseverance: "Yet doth [the parson] oftenest invite those, whom hee sees take best courses, that so both they may be encouraged to perservere, and others spurred to do well, that they may enjoy the like courtesie" (243:24–27). Herbert never recommends courtesy for courtesy's sake. Here, for instance, he suggests putting on a pleasant demeanor, not because one should simply be pleasant to another, but because of the opportunity for instruction that such behavior affords: "The Countrey Parson is generally sad . . . nevertheless, he sometimes refresheth himselfe, as knowing that nature will not bear everlasting droopings, and that *plesantnesse of disposi-*

tion is a great key to do good not onely because all men shun the company of perpetuall severity, but also for that when they are in company, *instructions seasoned with pleasantnesse, both enter sooner, and roote deeper"* (267:27–268:5, my italics). Herbert is convinced of the usefulness of courteous behavior. He writes: "There is much preaching in . . . friendliness" (284:21–22). And he assures his reader that in the ministry, "a pleasantness of disposition is of great use" (252:19).

While the ultimate aim of courtesy for the courtier is his own advancement, the aim of courtesy for Herbert is the "advancement" of his parish. That is, Herbert uses courtesy as a means of edifying his congregation. He recommends, for example, that in trying to win over sinners or heretics the parson find ways to show courtesies to the erring ones. The parson should employ: "a very loving and sweet usage of them, both in going to, and sending for them often, and in finding out Courtesies to place on them" (262:24–27). Alternatively, the withdrawal of courtesy is a useful tool for discouraging sinful behavior: "The Parsons punishing of sin and vice is . . . by withdrawing his bounty and courtesie from the parties offending" (254:22–23).

Teaching his congregation is the most common use Herbert makes of courtesy. He is especially careful to keep his discourses pleasing and courteous in order not to alienate his hearers. This effort to please one's hearers is a common theme of courtesy books. Here Castiglione explains how the courtier is to teach his prince, avoiding tediousness and offense: "In this way the Courtier will be able to lead his prince by the austere path of virtue, adorning it with shady fronds and strewing it with pretty flowers to lessen the tedium of the toilsome journey for one whose strength is slight; and now with music, now with arms and horses, now with verses, now with discourse of love . . . to keep his mind continually occupied in worthy pleasures, yet always impressing upon him also some virtuous habit along with these enticements, as I have said, beguiling him with salutary deception."[58] Like the courtier, Herbert's parson is to impress upon his people virtuous habits, beguiling them "with salutary deception." We have already noted the ways in which Herbert uses "all possible art" (232:31) to procure his congregation's attention while he preaches.[59] Herbert suggests theatrical manners and gestures, a "busy cast of his eye" (233:1), stories, sayings, and even tears to "lesson the tedium of the toilsome journey." Outside of church the parson is to continue this entertaining method. He agrees with Guazzo's dictum that "wittie and readie pleasantnesse delighteth wonderfully the hearers."[60] In "The Parson in Journey" Herbert advises his reader to mingle edification with pleasure when one begins conversing with a fellow traveler: "Therefore those [the parson] meets on the way he blesseth audibly, and with those he overtakes or that overtake him, hee begins some good discourses, such as may edify, interposing sometimes some short, and honest refreshments, which may make his other discourses more welcome, and lesse tedious" (251:2–6). "Short, and honest refreshments" are not recommended merely to delight the hearer, but to make the parson's theological discourses "more welcome and lesse tedious," or as Herbert puts it more graphically elsewhere, the parson, with his more didactic statements, "mingles other discourses for conversation sake, and to make his higher purposes slip the more easily" (249: 11–12).[61]

Thus while Herbert has "higher purposes" than the typical courtesy author, his method is surprisingly similar to theirs. He recommends using courtesy and liberality almost exclusively for their utilitarian functions, and these functions—to raise respect and esteem, to encourage dependence, and to make the parson's discourses more welcome to his hearers—raise unmistakable echoes from the pages of courtesy books. The very fact that Herbert chooses these two classical virtues of courtesy and liberality to describe the parson as well as justice, prudence, temperance, and courage rather than faith, hope, and charity or the fruits of the Spirit is significant. By choosing this particular set of virtues for his model parson Herbert directs his readers away from seeing *The Country Parson* as a common ministerial manual and toward viewing it in light of the courtesy tradition, thus underscoring the importance of appearances and shaking off "slovenliness" in the ministry.

The way Herbert recommends inculcating these virtues further connects his work to the courtesy tradition. As already noted, Herbert places much confidence in experience as a teacher.[62]

Comparatively, book-learning receives little praise in *The Country Parson*. We have also discovered that, as a clerical handbook, *The Country Parson* is unusual in this regard, since most other manual authors go to great lengths to insist on the need for humane learning in the ministry and even recommend page after page of reference works.[63] An explanation for this phenomenon suggests itself when we investigate the experience-vs.-text question in the courtesy tradition. Herbert's preference for experience seems to have its roots in a traditional, aristocratic convention.

Book-learning was certainly recommended by courtesy authors, but in the Renaissance courtesy world, scholarship was always the handmaiden of arms and civil service. Castiglione, for example, has been credited with encouraging education among the English nobles: "it is probable that his *Courtier* did more than any other one book to persuade the Elizabethan gentleman to unite learning to the courtly graces."[64] But as with liberality and courtesy, learning was extolled among courtesy authors chiefly for its practical value. Castiglione introduces his treatment of learning by mocking the French for their indifference toward letters: "the French recognize only the nobility of arms and reckon all the rest as nought . . . and they think that it is a great insult to call anyone a clerk."[65] But when Castiglione himself praises the knowledge of letters, he stresses "how *useful* and necessary to our life and dignity letters are," and he honors past heroes who added "the *ornament of letters* to valor in arms."[66] Castiglione recommends training in the humanities because, "in this way [the courtier] will never want for pleasant entertainment with the ladies, who are usually fond of such things";[67] and these studies, moreover, "will make him fluent, and bold and self-confident in speaking with everyone."[68]

Nevertheless, the educated courtier must always appear to prefer arms over letters, for arms are necessary to his rank, and letters merely a helpful addition: "[the courtier] should be always showing and esteeming arms as his chief profession and the other good accomplishments as ornaments thereto."[69] Osorius depicts the common belief that civil service is a more honorable aim than study for the nobleman. Here he voices his disapproval of the gentleman-scholar: "for neyther may they, which the rather to attayn knowledge and wysedom have abandoned all company and live in continuall studye be thought most worthye & honourable . . . for that they do not earnestly employ the benefit of their artes and sciences to the availe and commoditye of the common wealth."[70]

And the English courtesy author Peacham expresses the same opinion: "For since all Vertue consisteth in Action, and no man is borne for himselfe, we adde, beneficiall and usefull to his Country; for hardly they are to be admitted for Noble, who (though of never so excellent parts) consume their light, as in a darke Lanthorne, in contemplation, and a Stoicall retirednesse."[71] "All Vertue consisteth in Action"—this was the traditional code for the English aristocracy.[72] It was linked to the concept that the nobleman's task is to be "beneficiall and usefull to his Country." Thus the noble who spent his time in the pure pursuit of knowledge, "in contemplation, and a Stoicall retirednesse" was untrue to his class and calling.

If young nobles were not to be educated like clerks and scholars, how were they to be trained? As noted, book-learning made up a part of the training, though books were chosen according to their relative utility. The greater part of the nobles' education was to be based on experience. Kelso indicates that lesser members of the gentry might have to study thoroughly physic, divinity, or law in preparation for a vocation; nevertheless, "the gentleman, whether of higher or lower rank, must wear his learning with a difference, valuing it only as a part of his wisdom, the other and more important part to be gained from experience and not from books."[73]

This heavy reliance upon experience is reflected in the subject matter of courtesy books. Besides recommending the usual academic subjects, courtesy books devote most of their space to such topics as arms, wrestling, horsemanship, swimming, tennis, writing, and speaking,[74] drawing, painting, blazonry, carriage, travel, fishing,[75] carving, hunting, dancing, shooting the long bow,[76] eating, drinking, riding, running, leaping, hawking, and house-games.[77] The student is to gain proficiency in these gentlemanly arts, not by reading, of course, but by experience. Peacham's dictum, "all vertue consisteth of action," extended to the nobleman's education.

Most courtesy authors spelled out their confidence in the didactic value of experience quite clearly. In *The Courtier* Castiglione's Signor Gasparo asks this question: "I should like to know whether this instruction . . . ought to be begun as it were in daily practice and conduct . . . or whether one should begin by explaining . . . in short, whether [the young courtier's] mind must first be imbued and stamped with the virtues through reason and intelligence, or through practice." Signor Ottaviano responds, voicing Castiglione's own philosophy of education: "Just as in generation the body precedes the soul, so the irrational part of the soul precedes the rational. Hence, we must care for the body before the soul and for the appetite before the reason . . . for just as intellectual virtue is perfected by teaching, so moral virtue is perfected by practice. *First, therefore, we should teach through practice,* whereby it is possible to govern the appetites that are not yet capable of reason and direct them toward the good by way of such good exercise."[78] Antonio Guevara's statement on arms can be extended to all fields of gentlemanly interests and sums up the sentiments of the courtesy genre on the relative value of books and experience: "When amongst Knights or Gentlemen talke is of armes, a Gentleman ought to have great shame to say, that he read it, but rather that he saw it. For it is very convenient for the Philosopher to recount what hee hath read, but the Knight or gentleman it becommes to speake of things that hee hath done."[79]

If Herbert's own thinking is shaped by and shares this courtly preference for experience over text, and if Herbert is indeed trying to shape *The Country Parson* into a type of courtesy book, it is not surprising that *The Country Parson* would reflect such an insistent confidence in the didactic function of experience.[80] While Herbert's emphasis on such statements as "The Countrey Parson's Library is a holy Life" (278:11) make the work seem unusual among contemporary ministerial handbooks—recommending as they do libraries of actual texts—it strongly indicates how closely related is *The Country Parson* to the secular courtesy genre.[81]

In this chapter we have uncovered several significant ways in which *The Country Parson* resembles a secular courtesy manual: an acute awareness of social distinctions, its use of courtly metaphors, and its courtesy book subject matter—the instruction of nobles, the use the moral virtues, and the primacy of experience. Even the form of *The Country Parson*—literary and not homiletic—proves more like a courtesy book than a clerical manual. These likenesses begin to suggest an explanation for our earlier points of focus: Herbert's emphasis on life to the neglect of doctrine, his concern with outward appearances, and his preference for experience over scholarship.[82] A fuller explanation will present itself as we further investigate the use of appearances in the courtesy tradition and in one courtesy manual in particular, Stefano Guazzo's *The Civile Conversation*.

4
The Country Parson and *The Civile Conversation*

> I pray you tell mee what you thinke to bee the end
> and marke that wise and worthie men shoote at?
>
> —Stefano Guazzo,
> *The Civile Conversation*[1]

> I have resolved to set down the Form and Character
> of a true Pastour, that I may have a Mark to aim at.
>
> —George Herbert,
> *The Country Parson*[2]

THE PURPOSE OF THE COURTESY BOOK IS TO PROVIDE A MODEL FOR behavior, a "mark" at which the courtier, prince, or (as we shall see) even the aspiring pastor, may aim. For George Herbert and Stefano Guazzo, reaching this mark involves more than the mere successful manipulation of appearances, although it does include fashioning appearances. For both of these authors, the appropriate shaping of the outer man has wholesome spiritual effects both upon one's inner self and the inner selves of others. This chapter establishes a link between George Herbert and the Italian Renaissance courtesy author, Stefano Guazzo, and suggests that Guazzo's *The Civile Conversation* may have served as an inspiration for Herbert's *The Country Parson.* Despite near universal agreement that Herbert knew and used the methods of courtesy literature, no specific courtesy author has been suggested as a real inspiration or influence upon Herbert, in particular, for his pastoral manual, *The Country Parson.* There is, however, substantial evidence that points to Herbert's having read and admired Stefano Guazzo's *The Civile Conversation.* Examining this connection may illuminate some motivations for and strategies in *The Country Parson*.

Herbert would have had easy access to Guazzo's work. Along with Castiglione's *The Courtier* and Della Casa's *Galateo*, Guazzo's *The Civile Conversation* was one of the three great books of courtesy translated from the Italian that enjoyed immense popularity in sixteenth- and seventeenth-century England. Morris Tilley describes *The Civile Conversation* as "next to Castiglione's *Courtier* . . . probably the best known Italian book in England."[3] By 1586 any Englishman wishing to make Guazzo's acquaintance could choose from three Latin translations, two French, the original Italian, a revised Italian, George Pettie's English translation of Books I through III, and the Pettie-Young translation of Books I through IV.[4]

John Lievsay, in *Stefano Guazzo and the English Renaissance*, claims that "Guazzo and his work were thoroughly familiar to Elizabethan and Jacobean Englishmen" and produces an impressive list of literary references to *The Civile Conversation*.[5] Early in the last century Sir Edward Sullivan provided a detailed study of parallels between Shakespeare's plays and the Pettie-Young translation of *The Civile Conversation*. These parallels, Sullivan writes, "are so numerous, and are found so continuously through nearly the whole of Shakespeare's plays, that they cannot be accounted for on any rational basis of explanation without assuming that Shakespeare was a borrower from *The Civile Conversation*."[6] In addition to literary references, there is evidence of Guazzo's popularity from bookseller's catalogues, the *Stationer's Register*, and other miscellaneous manuscripts where Guazzo or *The Civile Conversation* (as it was known in England) is mentioned.[7]

Not only was *The Civile Conversation* enjoyed and discussed in society at large, but a member of Herbert's own family praises the work. In his *Autobiography* Herbert's eldest brother, Edward, interrupts his narrative to recommend Guazzo. Regarding a gentleman's recreation and behavior, he writes: "The exercises I wholly condemn are dicing and carding, especially if you play for any great sum of money . . . I could say much more concerning all these points of education, and particularly concerning the discreet civility which is to be observed in communication either with friends or strangers, but this work would grow too big; and that many precepts conducing thereunto may be had in *Guazzo de le The Civile Conversation.*"[8]

Guazzo's *The Civile Conversation,* then, was quite available to George Herbert, apparently on his own household shelf, and popular among writers of his era. We might speculate that the young George Herbert, interested as he was in the court, would have read this courtesy book as a matter of course. Happily, we can do more than simply speculate. Two important pieces of scholarship exist which, when linked together, point to George Herbert's having read and been familiar with Guazzo's *The Civile Conversation.* In summary, these studies demonstrate that George Herbert was the author of *Witts Recreations. Selected from the finest Fancies of Moderne Muses. With a Thousand Outlandish Proverbs* (1640), or, *Outlandish Proverbs,* and that the author of *Outlandish Proverbs* borrowed from *The Civile Conversation.*

F. E. Hutchinson provides a painstaking and convincing analysis of Herbert's connection with *Outlandish Proverbs.* He concludes that "the case for [Herbert] having formed at least the nucleus of the collection . . . is very strong."[9] And there is evidence that of those proverbs in the collection that had "not appeared in English dress before,"[10] Herbert may have found a substantial number in *The Civile Conversation.*[11] Lievsay contends that "Of the 1032 'outlandish' (i.e., foreign) proverbs at the end of Herbert's book, some fifty-odd are to be found in Guazzo's *The Civile Conversation* and *Dialoghi piacevoli.*"[12] Since some of these proverbs also appear in John Florio's *Second Fruites* (1591), Lievsay cautions, "it would be unwise to insist upon Guazzo as an immediate source."[13] Nevertheless, for fifteen of these fifty proverbs the Pettie-Young *The Civile Conversation* (1586) furnishes the earliest recorded instance in English literature and *Outlandish Proverbs* (1640) provides the second.[14] This evidence strongly suggests that the author of *Outlandish Proverbs* was familiar with Guazzo's *The Civile Conversation.* Lievsay adds in closing: "When it is remembered that these 'outlandish' proverbs are not drawn exclusively from the Italian, it will be seen that the high incidence of Guazzian proverbs is more striking than their bare number indicates."[15]

Anyone familiar with both *The Civile Conversation* and *The Country Parson* would not be surprised at the conclusion that George Herbert knew and apparently borrowed from Guazzo. The affinities between these works indicate an undeniable likeness of spirit that the authors share. It may be no coincidence that in his book, *Prayer and Power: George Herbert and Renaissance Courtship,* Michael Schoenfeldt makes more references to Guazzo than any courtesy author. (Schoenfeldt makes fourteen direct references to Guazzo. Castiglione, the next most frequently cited, receives eleven.) Most significantly, Herbert and Guazzo share a striking and unusual treatment of the important courtesy theme: "seeming and being." (This subject will be treated in some length in the following chapter.) It will be helpful first to examine three other noteworthy likenesses between *The Civile Conversation* and *The Country Parson*; these are a similar religious tone, a shared love for scripture and pious proverbs, and a concern for the doctrine and lives of their respective clergy.

The tone of both authors is clearly that of practical piety. Unique among continental courtesy book authors, Guazzo is ever concerned with the religious dimensions of his topics. *The Civile Conversation* is an undeniably Christian work. The other Italian courtesy books are thoroughly secular in comparison. It is difficult to imagine, for example, Della Casa or Castiglione recommending meekness and humility as Guazzo does: "God himselfe . . . withstandeth the proude, and sheweth mercy to the meeke and humble in heart" (1:101). But *The Civile Conversation* is replete with such affirmations of Christian orthodoxy. While Castiglione instructs men how to live well through the correct display of worldly appearances, Guazzo writes, "the wisedom of the world is folly with God. And it is a thing impossible for him to live well, who knoweth not God" (2:53). Della Casa and Machiavelli may tell a courtier how to take advantage of his servant, but Guazzo reminds the courtier of his "supreme mayster" and exhorts him "to intreate his inferiours, as he would bee intreated by his Superioures" (2:98, 109). Lievsay notes that "With Guazzo, religion is constantly emphasized as foundation for the rest of life, and Holy Writ is often invoked."[16] No other courtesy author quotes scripture with the same frequency and ease as does Guazzo. He makes use of the Bible with a naturalness that suggests a familiarity and even an intimacy with the text. For example, Guazzo condemns slanderers with a reference to the Epistle of James (3:1–8): "For now adaies men take such pleasure in this vice, that many which are free almost from all other faults, yet are they not able to bridle their blasphemous tongues" (1:65). Speaking of Socrates, but also alluding to Matthew 5:15, Guazzo writes: "For seeing al the Philosophers bent to the contemplation of nature, hee not only framed himselfe to get wisdome, to live wel, and to teach others to live, but gave himselfe altogether to the bringing to perfection this part of Philosophie . . . and made the worlde to see the open folly of those, who will rather hide a candel under a bushell, then to set it on a Candlestick" (1:32–33). Guazzo's knowledge of the Bible appears to be more than casual as he easily makes use of even relatively obscure texts, e.g., "Wo be to the lone man, who when he shalbe fallen downe, shall have none to helpe him up" (1:48; cf. Ecclesiastes 4:9–11). Guazzo stands out among courtesy authors with his copious scriptural quotations and allusions.

Herbert, of course, did not need a Guazzo to teach him to quote scripture. But Herbert undoubtedly would appreciate Guazzo's fondness for the Bible. Herbert's own love of the Old and New Testaments is everywhere apparent, and we can easily imagine Herbert finding an unexpected soul mate in Guazzo.[17] It is difficult to imagine Herbert taking Machiavelli or Castiglione or Della Casa, with their clearly secular purposes and strategies, as the inspiration for his "courtesy book." But Guazzo is different. Herbert would find *The Civile Conversation* delightful for the same reasons that many of his contemporaries did: for its respect for the scriptures and obvious spirit of piety.

In addition to quoting the Bible, *The Civile Conversation* makes abundant use of stories, anecdotes, and proverbs. Nearly every page uses one of these. Guazzo's work is a veritable mine of apothegms. Opening *The Civile Conversation* at random one is likely to find several proverbs:

> A friend of fooles wil become like unto them.
> Hee which toucheth pitch shalbe defiled therwith.

And as a dead coale, laied to a lively fire kindleth: so a naughty person meeting in companie with the good, partaketh with their conditions.
Out of the frying pan into the fire, or out of a fever into the hot evil.

(1:44–45)

Here again we can imagine Herbert finding delightful fellowship with Guazzo. We see in Herbert, as the author of *Outlandish Proverbs*, a love of apothegms. *The Country Parson* reinforces this impression, as in these representative proverbial phrases, which *The Country Parson* invokes:

For sins make all equall, whom they find together. (227:27)
The Choyce of his wife was made rather by his eare, then by his eye.* (238:26)
In the house of those that are skilld in musick, all are musicians. (240:30)
An old good servant boards a child. (241:10)
Prayers and provender never hinder journey. (251:14)
He that wil be respected, must respect. (268:23)
Do well, and right, and let the world sinke. (270:23)
None fouls his hands in his owne businesse.* (275:27)
If we would judge ourselves, we should not be judged; and if we would bound ourselves, we should not be bounded. (280:30)

These nine proverbs all appear in *The Country Parson*. (Those marked by an asterisk are also found in *The Civile Conversation*.)[18] Guazzo and Herbert are unique among courtesy writers for their judicious and generous use of such proverbs.

Finally, Guazzo and Herbert share an interest in a topic far removed from the concerns of other courtesy writers: the doctrine and lives of their nations' clergy.

Chapter 1 of this study explored Herbert's handling of the doctrine and life theme, concluding that—for a Protestant writer—Herbert places an unusual emphasis on the life or "good works" of a clergyman and is peculiar in his de-emphasis of correct doctrine. Chapters 2 and 3 explored this focus on the outer life and discussed Herbert's possible motives and models. The need associated with a particular audience constitutes a further motive. It seems likely that Herbert recognized a necessity for a courtesy book specifically designed for clergymen.

Reading the clerical manuals of Herbert's period, one cannot help but notice a recurring pair of grievances. Authors deplore both the contemporary state of piety among clergymen and the low esteem in which ministers were held by society. Cristina Malcolmson points to Herbert's concern for the reputation of the clergy in *The Country Parson* as part of her general argument for Herbert's "participation in the 'Protestant ethic' as well as his engagement in the world."[19] She also points out Herbert's awareness of the bad reputation of the clergy and his instructions to fellow clergymen to "fight it."[20] Ronald Cooley acknowledges that "one objective of [*The Country Parson*] is . . . to reduce . . . anti-clericalism."[21]

Herbert begins *The Country Parson* complaining about fawning chaplains who, "while they remember their earthly Lord, do much forget their heavenly; they wrong the Priesthood, neglect their duty, and [are] so farre from that which they seek with their over-submissivenesse, and cringings, that they shall ever be despised" (226:35–36). Yet later, in "The Parson in Contempt," Herbert gives advice to help the parson be less "despised" and regrets the "generall ignominy which is cast upon the profession" (268:10). Herbert was not alone in his time complaining about the low reputation of the clergy. In *The Worthy Church-Man* (1628), John Jackson calls ministers to "helpe to wash away the disrepute which stickes to our profession by those who startle at our want of learning or holinesse."[22] And yet he declares "let men thinke of us as meanely as they will, we are a chosen generation, and a royall Priesthood to him."[23] Richard Bernard begins his treatise *The Faithfull Shepheard* (1607) with a lament upon bad preachers: "Not a few unadvisedly take [preaching] in hand, speaking without judgement rashly, without order preposterously, teaching matter together without dependancie, little to the peoples edification, and lesse to the honour of the holy ordinance, which by these is made odious with many."[24] But shortly Bernard condemns noblemen who disdain the calling for themselves and their sons: "Some of our States and Gentrie, with prophane Esau contemne as he did this calling for a messe of pottage, worldly pompe, pleasure, and profit . . . Why . . . should any disdaine (o yee sonnes of Nobles) to take this calling upon you, or any of you to be malecontent, who have alredie entred hereunto, because the proud & wicked despise you?"[25] Comparing classical and Old Testament attitudes toward the priesthood with current ones, Bernard continues: "There is no cause why amongst us that are called Christians, [the priesthood] should be esteemed so contemptible a calling: which also the very heathen, who never knew the true God, so much reverenced . . . Uziah, a mightie King in Judah, who though he offended in presumption, yet his act declared his high esteeme of the Priests office, and that it was not so base in his eies as now the Ministerie of Christ is amongst many of us."[26] William Perkins also takes up the theme, first condemning the present state of the ministry: "Nor shall any mans case be so miserable, as an unconscionable Ministers: and though now such loose and licentious Ministers seeme to live in Jolitie, & without any feare, yet when God shall appeare . . . then will they cry out in fearefull anguish, Woe is mee, I am undone."[27] Perkins blames a lack of true conversion in England on a rash of unbelieving or unsanctified clergy: "In many places of our land, there is by God's blessing much teaching, yet ther is little reformation in the lives of the most . . . Where is the cause . . . many Ministers . . . unsanctified, & in their sins." And yet Perkins too deplores the "vile contempt" his contemporaries have for the ministry and he encourages pastors to consider the "high excellencie of their calling" in order to arm themselves "against the scorne and contempt of the world, which by wicked men is cast like dust and mire into the face of Ministers."[28]

This "contempt of clergy" theme is pervasive among seventeenth-century religious writers in England. Ronald Cooley describes the "lament for the state of the English clergy" as being a "perpetual refrain of sixteenth- and seventeenth-century English reformers."[29] They clearly felt that the contemporary ministry was particularly afflicted, both by the lives of its own members and the disrespect of outsiders. To what extent this phenomenon was real or imagined and to what extent the clergy brought the disdain of their contemporaries upon themselves is difficult to ascertain. The important point is that for Herbert and his colleagues there was a perceived problem in the ministry; and the problem was primarily related to the lives, not the doctrine of the clergy. Perkins here explains why so many people of his time were falling to "Atheisme" and "Papisme" and "foule sinnes": "Where is the cause? Surely not in the Gospel: nor in our doctrine, nor in the teaching of it: but one very principall cause is, many Ministers come into Gods presence unsanctified, & in their sins: not caring how loosely they live, in the face of their people; and therfore God in justice, though he instantly smite not them, with visible vengeance for their presumption: yet hee smites the people, with spirituall blindnesse, that they regard not their Doctrine, but looke at their lives, and doe rather follow the prophanenesse of the one, then the holinesse of the other."[30] For Perkins and most religious writers, the solution to this problem lay in a change of the offending ministers' hearts: "All ministers therefore, as they would see any fruite of their Ministerie, let them first sanctifie themselves, & clense their hearts by repentance."[31] Internalizing their doctrine would reform their lives. Herbert, however, approaches the problem completely differently and seeks to improve the parson's outer behavior.[32] Reading Guazzo could have provided Herbert with the inspiration for his particular response to the needs of the clergy.

The major part of *The Civile Conversation* (books 2 and 3) consists of discussions on how the gentleman should behave in nearly every conceivable social relationship: how the gentleman should relate to young men, old men, other gentlemen, yeomen, princes, magistrates, the learned, strangers, those in religious orders, women, wives, parents, children, widows, brothers, and servants. Most relationships are discussed fully and ample space is provided for the development of the topic. The relationship or "conversation" between the gentleman and the clergy, however, provides a glaring exception to this rule.[33] Conspicuous for its brevity, Guazzo's treatment of the "conversation between the secular and the religious" highlights the same contempt of clergy in sixteenth-century Roman Catholic Italy, which Herbert's contemporaries were bewailing in seventeenth-century Protestant England.

Guazzo begins by apologetically explaining why there is in fact so little "conversation" between priests and laymen. It seems that this sort of interaction "happeneth but one day in the yeere, and of that day but halfe houre only" spent in confessing sins

(1:230). Guazzo reluctantly admits that the reason gentlefolk "flie the conversation" of their "ghostly fathers" is the less-than-exemplary lives most of these clergymen lead. He makes the candid observation: "Lay men are for the most part of better life and conversation, than spiritual men are" (1:231). Guazzo admits that priests "by their doctrine they keepe us in the right," but we "must then leave it to God to judge of their life" (1:230–31). Guazzo devotes comparatively little space to the conversation of the clergy apparently in keeping with the rule that if he cannot find anything good to say, he will say nothing at all. (Since Guazzo is writing during the Counter-Reformation in Italy, there may have been other reasons for keeping his negative comments short.) Guazzo makes only this pious pronouncement: "God hath given [the clergy] unto us, not that we should be judges of their dooinges, but folowers of their doctrine" (1:230).

In his attention to the outer man, in his piety, his love of the scriptures and proverbs, and in his concern for the reputation of the clergy, Guazzo must have endeared himself to George Herbert. What better tribute to Guazzo could Herbert then have paid than to take up where *The Civile Conversation* left off? The life of the clergy obviously was a great concern of seventeenth-century English divines, as it was of Guazzo. But the religious were an audience that the typical Renaissance courtesy author either would not or dared not address. One can picture Herbert, upon finishing *The Civile Conversation,* resolving to write a courtesy book for one peculiar group of needy gentlemen: the clergy. Ronald Cooley rightly advises us to "understand *The Country Parson* as an exercise in professional, rather than personal, self-fashioning" and he confirms that "the ideal parson depicted . . . is a fabric of precepts of external behaviour."[34] Perhaps the Puritan manuals, focusing as they did on the pastor's conversion and heart and all but ignoring appearances, had not been entirely satisfactory to Herbert. Believing as he did in the efficacy of appearances, Herbert may have been inspired by Guazzo to help improve the clergyman's manner of life. Creating his manual along the lines of a courtesy book, instead of the more common sermon format, would be appropriate for Herbert's goal of addressing the need for attention to the outward appearances of the ministry.

Guazzo lamented over the clergy: "They ought . . . by their good life and doctrine to amend our naughtie lives" (1:231). But he is discouraged by the quality of their "conversation." Herbert, then, will show the clergy how to improve their "conversation" by providing an exemplary clergyman in his country parson, whose duty is "to do that which Christ did, and after his manner, both for Doctrine and Life" (225:19).

5
"Seeming and Being" in *The Country Parson*

"A man ought to indevour to bee suche a one,
as hee desireth to seeme to bee."
—Stefano Guazzo,
The Civile Conversation (1:155)

"Be what thou wouldst seeme to be."
—*Outlandish Proverbs* (No. 724)

If there is one theme that dominates the Renaissance courtesy genre, it is the relationship between "seeming" and "being." All courtesy writers, from the earliest Italian authors to the English Puritans are preoccupied with appearances in relation to reality. And while opinions vary widely regarding the purposes and aims of courtesy, the message of all courtesy books remains the same: appearances matter.

In the first chapter of this study we examined the theme of Herbert's *The Country Parson*, concluding that Herbert's chief concerns in this work are with the outer forms of the parson's life. Chapter 2 explored one possible explanation for this emphasis: Herbert's desire to steer a middle course between what he saw as Roman Catholic "superstition" and Puritan "slovenliness" regarding appearances in the ministry. Chapter 3 then initiated a comparison between *The Country Parson* and the courtesy manual, pointing out that while other authors of clerical handbooks chose the sermon model, Herbert's work is closer in spirit and focus to the secular courtesy book. Chapter 4 submitted Stefano Guazzo's *The Civile Conversation* as a possible influence and model for Herbert's "courtesy book." This chapter completes the comparison between *The Country Parson* and the courtesy tradition, focusing on the central courtesy theme of appearances and reality. Examining the treatment of "seeming and being" in several important courtesy treatises begins to reveal a satisfying explanation for Herbert's unusual choices regarding theme, subject matter, and genre in *The Country Parson.*

We have already noted that the stress in the typical clerical handbook is on the pastor's heart or inner self.[1] Such manuals concentrate on prayer, conversion (of the pastor first and then his people), a good conscience, appropriate feelings, holiness, the leading of the Holy Spirit, and acquiring the "tongue of the learned." While these works often discuss a pastor's duties toward his congregation, their chief interest is with the minister himself and his qualifications and preparedness for his calling. Since for most manualists, preparedness is largely a matter of the heart, most focus on the individual minister before God. The private self (the individual before God) rather than the public self (the individual in society) shapes the conventional clerical manual. These handbooks take their motto from the scripture text, "Man looks on the outward appearance, but the Lord looks on the heart."[2] Thus they typically say nothing or very little about the "seeming" or appearances of the pastor. Their concern is with his "being."

The focus of the courtesy book is entirely different from that of the clerical manual. Rather than the isolated self before God, the self in society or man before men is the subject of the courtesy book. Appearances play a significant role, and while "being" is not entirely ignored, "seeming" takes center stage.[3] This interest in appearances is most clearly articulated by the Italian courtesy authors. As J. L. Lievsay puts it, "Take moral soundings where you will in Machiavelli, Castiglione, or Della Case, what you acquire from these whited sepulchres resolves itself to this: It is better *to seem* than *to be*."[4] Ruth Kelso expressed the same thought more amiably: "like so many other beautiful things the ideal of beauty in the outward man, not of person but of ways, grew first on Italian soil."[5] While many imitators and adapters came later, the Italian Renaissance courtesy book was the prototype for all others. It is therefore instructive to compare the concept of appearances in Herbert with the ideals of some of the Italian "fathers of courtesy"—Baldesar Castiglione, Niccolò Machiavelli, Giovanni Della Casa, and Stefano Guazzo.[6] *The Country Parson* seems to take its inspiration from two concepts central to the theme of "seeming" in these works: fashioning the public self and using "art" to achieve appropriate appearances.

Just as surely as clerical handbooks attempted to shape and improve the inner man, courtesy books existed to fashion the outer man, the man that others saw, the man in society. More vividly than the others, Machiavelli depicts the great gulf that can exist between appearances and reality. In this passage emphasizing the importance of the prince's public image, for example, he acknowledges the distance between seeming and being:

> I know everyone will agree that among these many qualities a prince certainly ought to have all those that are considered good. But since it is impossible to have and exercise them all . . . a prince must be shrewd enough to avoid the public disgrace of those vices that would lose him his state. If he possibly can, he should also guard against vices that will not lose him his state; but if he cannot prevent them, he should not be too worried about indulging them. And furthermore, he should not be too worried about incurring blame for any vice without which he would find it hard to save his state. For if you look at matters carefully, you will see that something resembling virtue, if you follow it, may be your ruin, while something else resembling vice will lead, if you follow it, to your security and well-being.[7]

Throughout *The Prince* Machiavelli insists that one must "be shrewd enough" to create a good public image, but one "should not be too worried about indulging" one's private vices. "It is better to seem than to be" is the code of Machiavelli's work. While other courtesy authors may not so candidly admit such indifference to true virtue, the clear message of their works is the same: seeming takes precedence over being.

Further, Della Casa explains how impotent real virtue is without the proper "fashions, gestures, and manners." The man in society thus will do well to carefully fashion his appearances: "who so disposeth himselfe to live, not in solitarie and deserte places, as Heremites, but in fellowship with men . . . will think it a very necessarie thing, to have skill to put himselfe forth comely and seemely, in his fashions, gestures and manners; the lacke of which parts doth make those other vertues lame, and litle or nothing can they work to good effect, without other helpes: wheare this civilite and courtesie, without other releefe or patrimonie, is riche of it selfe, & hath substance enough."[8]

Della Casa goes on to explain, "It is not inoughe for a man, to doe things that be good: but hee must also have a care, hee doe them with a good grace."[9] Merely "being good" apparently cannot compete with also "looking good."

Perhaps better than anyone else, Castiglione describes how to fashion the outer man and to do things "with a good grace." He emphasizes that the courtier is to make use of every opportunity to create the appealing public image. Here Castiglione suggests how the courtier might use an interest in music to his advantage: "Therefore, let the Courtier turn to music as to a pastime, and as though forced. And although he may know and understand what he does, in this also I would have him dissimulate the care and effort that is required in doing anything well; and let him appear to esteem but little this accomplishment of his, yet by peforming it excellently well, make others esteem it highly."[10]

The courtier may work hard at perfecting his knowledge or skill, but he should appear to excel naturally, without effort; this is to do things with style and to create the proper impression: "let [the courtier] have the discretion and good judgment to know how to bring people adroitly and opportunely to see and hear what he considers himself to excel in, always seeming to do this without ostentation, casually as it were, and rather when begged by others than because he wishes it. And in everything that he has to do or say, let him, if possible, always come prepared and ready, but give the appearance that all is done on the spur of the moment. But as for those things in which he feels himself to be mediocre, let him touch on them in passing, without dwelling much upon them, though in such a way as to cause others to think that he knows much more about them than he lays claim to know."[11] *The Prince, The Galateo,* and *The Book of the Courtier* all teach and urge their readers to fashion effective appearances.

This kind of advice could not be more opposed to the advice of Herbert's contemporaries writing clerical handbooks. While Machiavelli, Della Casa, and Castiglione encourage their readers to create the perfect public image, most English clerical authors deemphasize the importance of appearances and go so far as to say that the godly minister will denounce any compliments and even point out his own defects. Perkins explains: "godly Ministers finde fault with themselves, when other men cannot, and cry out against themselves, for their pollution . . . when no other man can accuse them of the least crime: nay, when others doe magnifie God for his graces on them, and praise their giftes, and commend their good lives, even then doe they condemne themselves, and exclaime against their owne corruptions; and their owne smallest negligences, or omissions, are great woundes to their consciences; & their last sines, and their most pardonable infirmities, are fore buthrens unto them: for of all men in the worlde, a godly Minister is a man of the most tender conscience.[12]

Such self denigration is anathema to the courtesy author. Castiglione, for example, calls it "folly" to willingly admit ignorance of anything, accuse, or depreciate oneself in any way.[13] This is because courtesy authors are interested in creating a perfect exterior; the courtier's inner life is not their concern. The clerical manualists, however, are suspicious even of an apparently "perfect" outer man. They call for soul searching and confession even "when no other man can accuse them of the least crime."

When *The Country Parson* is compared both to the contemporary clerical manual and the Renaissance courtesy book, there is no doubt of which spirit it partakes. Unlike other authors of pastoral handbooks, Herbert never calls on the minister to humble himself in the eyes of others; he never discusses such intimate concerns as the pastor's conversion, his conscience, his personal prayer life, or his attention to the Holy Spirit. Private issues are replaced by public ones regarding the minister before his congregation. Like the courtesy authors, Herbert's concern in *The Country Parson* is with a man in society, and his focus is on improving his public image.

As we have seen, the great bulk of Herbert's advice is not overtly linked to spiritual realities, but to the minister's appearances. Herbert writes, for example, that the parson must master patience and mortification, not because this is necessary for his inner life but because of the effect such practices have on his "seeming": these are "the two highest points of Life, wherein a Christian is most seen" (227:4). Herbert warns against "luxury" because it is a "very visible sin" (227:22). And he shows his courtesy-like concern with his public image in recommendations like this one: "Yet . . . he labours most in those things which are most apt to scandalize his Parish" (227:11). When Herbert suggests certain techniques for preaching, he does so with the assurance that such techniques "carry great holiness in them" and will make the sermon "appear exceeding reverent, and holy" (234:1, 24). His interest in the parson's appearances is clear as he recommends certain courteous dialogues after which he comments, "such discourses shew very Holy" (234:36).[14] *The Country Parson* apparently has more to say about how to "shew" holy than how to be holy. And while Herbert is neither advocating the blatant duplicity of *The Prince* nor undervaluing virtue as in *The Galateo* or *The Courtier,* he is clearly recommending the sort of positive self-fashioning peculiar to the courtesy book and foreign to the clerical manual.

The method which they recommend for creating the proper public man constitutes a further likeness between Herbert and the Italian authors. Both Herbert and the Italians advise using a kind of crafting of seeming or what they call "art" to achieve their desired ends. Machiavelli again provides the most direct illustration. Here he suggests artfully fashioning one's appearances while disregarding any contradictory realities:

> In actual fact, a prince may not have all the admirable qualities we listed [mercy, truthfulness, humanity, sincerity, and piety], but it is very necessary that he should seem to have them . . . when you just seem to have them, they are useful. It is good to appear merciful, truthful, humane, sincere, and religious. . ..To preserve the state, he often has to do things against his word, against charity, against humanity, against religion. Hence a prince should take great care never to drop a word that does not seem imbued with the five good qualities noted above; to anyone who sees or hears him, he should appear all compassion, all honor, all humanity, all integrity, all religion. Nothing is more necessary than to seem. Everyone sees what you seem to be, few know what you really are.[15]

Such advice, while it reflects a philosophy central to the courtesy genre, seems too blatantly non-Christian for even some of the pillars of the courtesy tradition. Thus Castiglione deems it necessary occasionally to justify his artfulness. Here, for example, Signor Federico defends (against charges of deception made by Signor Gaspar) the courtier who makes others believe he knows more than he does in fact know:

> Then Signor Gaspar Pallavicino replied: "This seems to me to be not an art, but an actual deceit; and I do not think it seemly for anyone who wishes to be a man of honor ever to deceive."
>
> "This," said messer Federico, "is an ornament attending the thing done, rather than deceit; and even if it be deceit, it is not to be censured. Will you also say that, in the case of two men who are fencing, the one who wins deceives the other? He wins because he has more art than the other. And if you have a beautiful jewel with no setting, and it passes into the hands of a good goldsmith who with a skillful setting makes it appear far more beautiful, will you say that the goldsmith deceives the eyes of the one who looks at it? Surely he deserves praise for that deceit, because with good judgment and art his masterful hand often adds grace and adornment to ivory or to silver or to a beautiful stone by setting it in fine gold. Therefore let us not say that art—or deceit such as this, if you insist on calling it that—deserves any blame.[16]

Castiglione explains that crafting one's outer appearances, even if they are purely show, deserves praise if it "adds grace and adornment" to the individual. Later he calls such artfulness "circumspect dissimulation"[17] and "salutary deception."[18] The whole of *The Courtier,* in fact, instructs the reader on how to artfully appear—in speaking, eating, recreation, apparel, gestures, and carriage—regardless of whether the courtier's being actually matches his seeming. Della Casa emphasizes the painstaking effort required to so hone one's manners and fashions, implying that proper appearances are generally formed against one's true nature: "It is not inough to have knowledge and Art, in matters concerning manners and fashions of men: But it is needefull withall, to worke them to a perfect effect, to practise and use them muche: which cannot be had uppon the soudaine, nor learned by & by: but it is number of yeares that must winne it."[19]

To work one's manners "to a perfect effect" is indeed an "art" and not something that naturally flows from one's being, nor is it necessarily reflective of one's true self. But this is not the concern of the courtesy book author.

Making one's outer man a reflection of one's inner man is, however, the concern of the clerical manualist. While Della Casa and Castiglione devote page after page to the "how to's" of proper manners—touching every subject from how to blow one's nose without offense to how to address one's prince—the authors of pastoral handbooks give instructions on enhancing the mind and the spirit. The only interest these divines have with the outer man is as it is a reflection of the inner. William Perkins provides a typical example of this attitude. Here he briefly comments on the same topics to which a courtesy author would devote chapters: "a Minister cannot be too carefull in his calling, in his words, dyet, companie, recreation, apparell, gestures, and in his whole cariage, because little sinnes are so great in them."[20] The reason a courtier must be careful about his words, diet, company, and so on is because of the way they might contribute or detract from the appearance he is trying to create. Perkins's minister, contrarily, is careful about such things because of the occasions for sin they represent.

In light of this contrast, it is significant that Herbert's *The Country Parson* is so interested in the artful manipulation of appearances and apparently less interested in the parson's heart. "The Parson preaching," unlike comparable contemporary treatises on preaching, tells the pastor how to shape appearances effectively from the pulpit.[21] Herbert recommends using "all possible art" to properly affect one's auditors: "When [the parson] preacheth, he procures attention *by all possible art,* both by earnestnesse of speech, it being naturall to men to think, that where there is much earnestness, there is somewhat worth hearing; and by a diligent, and busy cast of his eye on his auditors, with letting them know, that he observes who marks and who not. By these and other means the Parson procures attention" (232:30–233:22, my italics).

Herbert goes on in this chapter to coach the pastor in pulpit performance: how to gaze out over the congregation, what words to say, and how to weave emotion and even tears into the sermon. "The Parson praying" likewise focuses, not on the heart, but on the "art" of prayer. Herbert suggests using effective looks, gestures, and speaking techniques, what Castiglione would call "circumspect dissimulation," to impress his hearers, because "no Sermon moves them so much to a reverence, which they forget againe, when they come to pray, as a devout behaviour in the very act of praying" (231:14–16, my italics.)[22] Unlike Perkins, who shows an interest in the pastor's appearances because "little sinnes are so great" in the minister's life, Herbert is concerned with the *public response* to one's appearances: "[The pastor] is very circumspect in all companyes, both of his behaviour, speech, and very looks, knowing himself to he both suspected, and envyed" (237:13–15). As we can see, like the courtesy authors, Herbert extends his suggestion to use "all possible art" beyond speech and behavior. His concern with appearances touches such standard courtesy topics as apparel, eating, and surroundings.

Castiglione suggests that choosing appropriate clothing is part of the courtier's "art," because the courtier can use this means to shape the public's view of him: "[The courtier] ought to consider what appearance he wishes to have and what manner of man he wishes to be taken for, and dress accordingly; and see to it that his attire aid him to be so regarded even by those who do not hear him speak or see him do anything whatever."[23]

Similarly, Herbert suggests that the parson's attire can be used to show "what manner of man" he is: "The Parsons . . . apparell [is] plaine, but reverend, and clean, without spots, or dust, or smell; the purity of his mind breaking out, and dilating it selfe even to his body, cloaths, and habitation" (228:10–13). By this Herbert does not mean, of course, that one's mind literally "breaks out" and spills itself onto one's exterior, a pure mind somehow laundering one's clothing. He is instead advising that the pastor dress so that his clothes proclaim the supposed state of his mind: clean and without spot. The parson's exterior helps him to be seen as the kind of man "he wishes to be taken for." While other divines would agree that one should dress in a manner fitting his calling, none gives this kind of care and attention to the parson's apparel. Other manualists want clothes merely to be appropriate; Herbert wants them to have an effect.

The sole ethic of *The Galateo* is to please others, "to win their good graces and one's own ultimate success . . . to perform every act with an eye to its effect on those about us."[24] In giving instructions on how to behave at meals, then, Della Casa uses this rule: If "the company is muche offended" by one's behavior, one's behavior is inappropriate.[25] Herbert too makes the response of others important in determining one's behavior at table. Rather than condemning gluttony with scriptural injunctions and explaining the harm such a sin might do to one's soul, for example, Herbert makes its effect on those about him a rule of thumb for table manners. Sounding like a page out of any number of courtesy books, this passage from Herbert reveals his interest in "artful" eating: "hee that eats offensively to the Company, either in his order, or length of eating, is scandalous and uncharitable" (266:10–11). With no mention of the spiritual causes or effects of gluttony, Herbert reasons that men must eat "neither to the disturbance of their health, nor of their affairs . . . nor of their estate, nor of their brethren" (266:13–17). Such advice seems more likely to be found in a manual for gentlemen than one for parsons. The opinion of others, rather than biblical guidelines, guides the parson's table manners.

Even one's surroundings and possessions can become material for artful self-fashioning. Machiavelli and Castiglione both explain the importance of creating about oneself an aura of majesty and wealth. Castiglione, for example, writes: "[The Courtier] ought to offer magnificent banquets, festivals, games, public shows; and have a great many fine horses for use in war and for pleasure in time of peace, falcons, dogs, and all the other things that pertain to the pleasures of great lords."[26]

He urges the great man to build monuments to himself and so shape his appearances even for future generations: "I should also try to induce him to build great edifices, both to win honor in his lifetime and to leave the memory of himself to posterity."[27]

Herbert too is interested in artfully shaping those things that surround the parson and that may reflect his character. Unlike other writers of clerical handbooks, Herbert shows great concern for the appearances of his house and furniture (241:11–15) and especially his church (246–47). But while Castiglione and the other courtesy authors recommend fashioning one's surroundings largely for selfish ends ("to win honor in [one's] lifetime"), Herbert does not. Herbert is creating a connection between *The Country Parson* and the mainstream courtesy tradition, but his purposes in fashioning the public self and using "all possible art" ultimately differ from those of the founders of the tradition.

For Machiavelli appearances matter because one must use them to gain power. For Della Casa appearances help one to please significant people. For Castiglione appearances generate praise for the courtier. The way to power, to please, and to praise—appearances are the avenue to such ends for the secular courtesy writers. That is, they are for all but one of the great Italian courtesy authors, Stefano Guazzo. Guazzo's purposes regarding seeming and being are significantly different from those of his compatriots and strikingly akin to Herbert's. Let us examine *The Civile Conversation* and *The Country Parson,* then, on these two important courtesy themes: using "all possible art" and fashioning a public self.

Guazzo's *The Civile Conversation* is every inch a courtesy book in its concern for appearances and its promoting "art" to enhance those appearances. Sounding very much like a devoted disciple of Castiglione, Guazzo here describes the artful manipulation of appearances as the duty of the courtier: "the dutie of a perfect Courtier . . . is to do all things with carefull diligence, and skilfull art: mary yet so that the art is hidden, and the whole seemeth to be doone by chaunce, that he may thereby be had in more admiration."[28] Later Guazzo suggests that we must artfully handle those who delude us: "now we see, that [our enemy] biddeth us good morrowe with his mouth, which wisheth us much sorowe in his heart. But what will you have a man doe? We must by their example give them mery lookes, and . . . must play the Foxe with Foxes, and delude art, with art."[29]

Guazzo clearly promotes the shaping of appearances. Like other courtesy writers, he gives specific advice on effective speaking and gestures and facial expression. But unlike Machiavelli, Castiglione, and Della Casa, his purpose is not merely to help the courtier "thereby be had in more admiration"; rather, his intent has more to do with the courtier's audience than the courtier himself. For example, Anniball (the character in *The Civile Con-*

versation who most often speaks for Guazzo) explains that the courtier should polish his language with rhetoric, philosophy, and whatever "good giftes" he can: "I would have him aide nature with a little art, and seeke to furnish himself with such good giftes, that he make himselfe place, bee disired, honoured, and esteemed in any honest companie hee shall come in."[30]

But while Guazzo is content to have his courtier admired, this is not the primary reason for suggesting that he aid nature with art. Anniball goes on to explain that the courtier is not merely interested a improving his own image, but that his goal is to affect the hearts and minds of his auditors: "our chiefe labour must bee to moove the heartes of the hearers; and wee must weigh this, that nothing can enter into their hearts, which is not currantly spoken, and without offence to the eares: and therefore wee must labour to have . . . a comely grace in holding our peace, and a lively force in speaking."[31]

Speech, says Anniball, should be used to touch the heart of another, and this can best be done by choosing fashionable phrases (that "which is . . . curranty spoken"), by pleasing the ear, and by using "comely grace" and "lively force." Guazzo suggests sprinkling one's speech with "Sentences, pleasant Jestes, Fables, Allegories, Similitudes, Proverbes, Comptes, and other delightful speache, varying from the common fourme or talke," because such things "hath no small force to content the hearers." And "therefore," Guazzo continues, "it is needefull to aide ourselves with a litle Art."[32]

Conspicuously unlike the other Italian authors, Guazzo suggests using such art, not primarily for self-aggrandizement, but for moving the hearts of men.

Guazzo further recommends developing a kind of stage presence for speaking and explains that one ought to "take paine in" perfecting it because "for that the aide of the speaker, [is] to stirre up the affections of others."[33] Having said that, Guazzo provides illustrations of two who perfected such a presence: "Apuleius . . . was judged most eloquent, for his countenance, gesture, and comely mooving of the body, with the which good partes, hee more allured his auditours, then with copie of wordes. lt is saide further, that Hortensius tooke more paines in trimming up his body, then in framing of his speache: so that it was doubtful whether men ranne rather to heholde him, then to heare him."[34]

Like the other Italian courtesy authors, Guazzo urges his courtier to use art in "countenance, gesture, and comely mooving of the body." Unlike the others, Guazzo's purpose is to "stir'e up the affections of others." If Machiavelli or Castiglione had recommended similar behavior, their purposes would be clear. They would surely advise moving others' affections for the benefit of the courtier, so that he would be more loved and admired and thereby better served.[35] But Guazzo's purpose in thus touching his hearers is remarkably different. Guazzo urges the courtier to "stirre up the affections of others,' not primarily for the courtier's good, but for the ultimate good of his hearers: "I say then, that our tongue shall bring foorth wordes which shall have force to stirre up mens mindes . . . *in godlinesse and goodnesse*."[36] Guazzo is the only major Italian courtesy author who has as his object not merely the worldly advancement of the gentleman or courtier, but also the improvement of the courtier's heart and the edification of others.

Herbert, like Guazzo and the other Italians, suggests using "all possible art" on an audience. He recommends sprinkling one's talk with "Fables, Allegories, Similitudes . . . and other delightfull speache." Here Herbert describes the successful parson preaching: "Sometimes he tells them stories, and sayings of others, according as his text invites him; for them also men heed, and remember better then exhortations . . . but stories and sayings they will well remember" (223:11–18).

Unlike the Puritan manual authors, Herbert does not restrict his parson to using biblical examples; he encourages the preacher artfully to weave fables, stories, and sayings of others into his speech. But this "art" is categorically unlike that employed by Castiglione, Machiavelli, and Della Casa, for Herbert's purpose in such ornamentation is not to make the parson to "thereby be had in more admiration." Herbert's intent instead has more to do with the congregation than the parson. It is to do good to his hearers. Here Herbert suggests mixing didactic discourse with lighter speech, perhaps stories or jests, in order to edify his interlocutors: "Therefore those he meets on the way he blesseth audibly, and with those he overtakes or that overtake him, hee begins good discourses, such as may edify, interposing sometimes some short, and honest refreshments, which may make his other discourses more welcome, and lesse tedious (251: 2–6).

As Guazzo recommends that "there be a little labour bestowed in the action, jesture, and pronouncing of the woordes," Herbert likewise suggests certain gestures, tone of voice, and expression to "stirre up mens mindes . . . In godlinesse and goodnesse." In order to "affect . . . his people" (231:13) Herbert recommends to the parson an appropriate stage presence. When the parson is to read divine services, for example, Herbert instructs him to compose "himselfe to all possible reverence; lifting up his heart and hands, and eyes, and using all other gestures which may expresse a hearty, and unfeyned devotion" (231:2–3). And he provides specific instructions on how to bestow "a little labour" in the "pronouncing of the woordes": "his voyce is humble, his words treatable, and slow yet not so slow neither, as to let the fervency of the supplicant hang and dy between speaking, but with a grave livelinesse, between fear and zeal, pausing yet pressing" (231:16–20).

Such attention to the art of praying is rarely, if ever, shown by Herbert's fellow manualists, who choose instead to focus or the content, not the aesthetics of the service. But like Guazzo, Herbert's concern for appearances is more altruistic than that of the typical courtesy author. Herbert wants to stir up the parson's congregation, and he wants to instill knowledge in his hearers. He clearly desires the parson to "inflame this knowledge, to presse, and drive it to practice, turning it to reformation of life, by pithy and lively exhortations" (255:5–7). The parson's "art" is meant to reform the hearts and lives of the hearers. In his prayer before the sermon the parson prays: "O make thy word a swift word, passing from ear to the heart, from the heart to the life and conversation" (289:29–30). While he prays that God's word would transform the heart and "conversation" of his people, Herbert does not rely solely on the power of the spoken Word, but believes that the parson must preach the Word with "all possible art" (232:31). Herbert shares with Guazzo a spiritual strategy for artful self-fashioning. A shared philosophy of the public self, then, is not surprising.

Like that of all courtesy authors, Guazzo's subject is the man in society, not the isolated individual or the man before God. Unlike other courtesy authors, Guazzo is not content simply to assume the worthiness of his topic. Rather, he makes his reasons for treating the public man quite clear in a long introductory argument on the importance of "civil conversation." By "conversation" Guazzo does not mean mere discourse, although discourse is a part of conversation. The modern English "conversation" does not convey Guazzo's idea, but the Renaissance English, reflected in this verse from the Authorized Bible (1611) does: "Having your conversation honest among the Gentiles, that . . . They may by your good works which they shall behold, glorifie God in the day of visitation."[37] A typical modern translation of the verse begins, "Maintain good conduct among the Gentiles."[38] "Conversation" signifies one's outward manner of life, including speech and behavior. "Civil conversation" specifies one's public conduct or conduct among others, as contemporary readers of Guazzo—both Italian and English—would have understood.

In his apology for treating civil conversation, Guazzo makes clear the kind of behavior his book will advocate: "Too bee shorte, my meaning is an honest commendable and vertuous kinde of living in the world."[39] Guazzo's topic is neither the virtuous individual before God (the subject of the clerical manual) nor the amoral (or immoral) courtier in society (the subject of most courtesy books). He is interested instead in fashioning an "honest commendable and vertuous" man "living in the world."[40] By "vertuous" Guazzo refers to having a mixture of both the classical and Christian virtues. In *The Civile Conversation* he specifically recommends these: wisdom, justice, fortitude, and temperance,[41] piety, and charity.[42] Despite the longer list of pagan virtues *The Civile Conversation* is a thoroughly Christian work. In this regard *The Civile Conversation* differs sharply from the other Italian courtesy books. Lievsay's comparison between Guazzo and Castiglione locates Guazzo's place among the other authors of the genre: "Castiglione, who died in the service of the Church, allows hardly a breath of Christian doctrine, much less of Christian spirit, to sully the pages of his essentially pagan work. For him, God is in exile—or at least in abeyance. With Guazzo, religion is constantly emphasized as foundation for the rest of life, and Holy Writ is often invoked. No doubt this careful morality, this gentle, unfeigned, decent, and obvious piety was one of the factors which rendered this book so acceptable to Elizabethan Englishmen, a breed not highly tolerant of things Catholic."[43]

When Guazzo recommends public self-fashioning, then, we can expect his presuppositions for it to be radically different from what we have come to expect from the typical courtesy author. And they are. As we look closely at *The Civile Conversation,* we find that Guazzo, in fact, "baptizes" public self-fashioning to make it congenial to his pious purposes. In doing so he may also have made the art of self-fashioning congenial to George Herbert's purposes as well.

The first aspect of public self-fashioning that Guazzo sanctifies is the courtesy book emphasis on the public man, the man in society. His long introductory discussion on civil conversation is largely an apology for Guazzo's attention to societal man rather than the individual soul. The argument assumes the form of a dialogue between Guazzo's ailing brother, William, and his friend and doctor, Anniball. Anniball, clearly the conveyer of the author's opinions, defends the virtues of civil conversation, or "an honest, commendable, and vertuous kind of living in the world" against the attacks of William who prefers solitary study and contemplation to social intercourse. To the degree that this discussion shows a preference for the active life over the contemplative as appropriate to the gentleman, it is standard courtesy book fare. But Guazzo's religious apology is far from typical.

Guazzo defends the public life as necessary for salvation and spiritual health. Among other arguments, Anniball puts this one forward: "Conversation is necessary. For you cannot go to visite the sicke, to releeve the poore, to correct and admonishe your brother, to comfort the afflicted, if you remain alwaies mewed up."[44] He further argues: "you know we must enter into the kingdome of heaven through tribulations and troubles. And although hee do wisely, who, to fly the combat of the fleshe against the spirit, retireth into some obscure and solitarie place, yet consider the great virtue and singular merite of him, who being placed in the midst of pleasurs, forbeareth them, and maketh a conquest of him selfe."[45]

The rhetoric of spiritual warfare here is remarkable. Sounding more like a portion of a Pauline Epistle than a courtesy book, this dialogue recommends the public life as an arena for combat between flesh and spirit and conquest of the self. The gentleman must participate in society, not for worldly advancement or even civil service, but for opportunities for Christian charity and spiritual battle.

Anniball further explains that we have the example of Christ's civil conversation to inspire us: "And if . . . Christ . . . had not been conversable, it had not gone well with us: for that disputing, preaching, healing the sicke, making the blinde to see, raysing the dead to life hee was conversant amongst us . . . and in the ende shed his innocent blood for our redemption."[46]

In making Christ a courtesy exemplar, Guazzo emphasizes how far he is from the secular spirit and imagination of the traditional courtesy book. *The Civile Conversation,* in keeping with its genre, constantly recommends ways to improve the outer man, but (as we shall see) this is always done with a view to its relationship to spiritual realities. For Guazzo, Christ is the perfect embodiment of "seeming and being"; that is, Christ's outer appearances and inner realities were perfect reflections of one another.

Among other arguments Guazzo includes one which maintains that even self-knowledge, the most intimate subject of all inquiry, is dependent upon public intercourse. As a result of civil conversation, one may come to know himself and thereby correct his own faults: "by meanes of civil conversation, a man may not only cleere himselfe of cowardly abjection, and vaine presumption, but besides, cloath himselfe with the knowledge of himselfe. For if you consider it wel, the judgement which wee have to knowe our selves, is not ours, but wee borrow it of others: for so much as when wee are by divers persons advertised, blamed, reproved . . . at the length we are content to submit our selves some imperfection, which wee indevour to correct after other mens judgement."[47]

"Our judgements, and the knowledge of our selves," Anniball continues, "dependeth on the judgement and conversation of many."[48] Guazzo recommends the public life for strikingly ethical reasons—for the correction of faults in oneself and in others:

"God hath made man a companable creature, that by meanes of Conversation, hee may both assist others, and bee assisted him selfe, as neede shall require."[49]

Guazzo goes as far as to assert that civil conversation can heal the sick body, mind, and soul. At the end of the long discourse between William and Anniball, which makes up the bulk of Guazzo's book, William admits that civil conversation is indeed better than solitude and that, in fact, his three-day "civil conversation" with Anniball has healed him. William thankfully says to his friend: "I am alreadie certified, of the great and marvaillous fruits which bud from the tree of The Civile Conversation, in so much if you have not onelie disposed my understanding . . . but by meanes also of your sweet companie, I doe sensiblie feele all the superfluous humours (engendred by solitarinesse) consumed quite, and spent in mee, so that I may now say to have (as it wer) obtained that, which the Prophet did desire, that is, a cleane heart, an upright spirit."[50]

Quoting from Psalm 51, William rejoices that civil conversation has healed him, physically and spiritually. Guazzo here suggests that social interaction or civil conversation can do that which is more commonly believed to be the result of private communion with God: cleansing of the soul. Guazzo teaches that the public life can some how make one righteous. While not negating the inner life, Guazzo thus reveals a high view of social intercourse and the influence of the outer man on the inner.

Among other claims, then, Guazzo maintains that civil conversation is at least in part responsible for spiritual health and salvation, self-knowledge and improvement, and healing of the body, mind, and soul. These extraordinary claims give enormous spiritual significance to civil conversation. In thus baptizing social intercourse, Guazzo provides religious justification for the courtesy book's focus on the public self.

Guazzo provides a remarkable parallel to Herbert who likewise finds immense religious significance in "civil conversation." While social intercourse, or "living in the world" as it has often been called, is nothing new in Christian theology, *The Country Parson's* emphasis on and treatment of the pastor's public self is unusual among works of its genre. Herbert's attention to the outer man is subtly justified by its possibilities for spiritual impact.

As noted earlier, *The Country Parson* stands out among clerical manuals of its time for its persistent focus on the minister's public self: his outer life, appearances, and works.[51] It would certainly be untrue to say that the other manualists never mention the pastor's public life. They are in fact concerned that the minister "walks worthily of his calling," and on occasion they warn the pastor of his need to be an example to the flock. Nevertheless, there exists an unmistakable difference in emphasis. Other manualists concentrate their instructions on the parson's calling, his private prayer, his attention to the Holy Spirit, his studies, and personal spiritual battles. Courtesy authors have the opposite focus, an outward and social one. *The Courtier* describes how the gentleman should behave with commoners, women, other gentlemen, magistrates, and his prince. Machiavelli prescribes for the prince various behaviors to be exhibited with counselors, enemies, soldiers, and ordinary citizens. Guazzo instructs his reader by laying out the proper behavior among these groups: young and old, gentlemen and yeomen, rulers and private citizens, learned and ignorant, strangers and residents, secular and religious, and gentlemen and women. Herbert's instructions—like those in a courtesy manual—likewise concentrate upon the man in various social relationships: the parson and his wife, children, and servants ("The Parson in his House"); the parson and the poor ("The Parson's Charity"); the parson with confused and heretical parishioners ("The Parson Arguing"); the parson and those outside his parish ("The Parson in Journey"); the parson with carnal members of his flock ("The Parson Punishing" and "The Parson in Contempt"); "The Parson with His Church Wardens," and so on. Like the courtesy author, Herbert devotes the bulk of his work, not to the private spiritual life, but to giving instructions on how to behave in a variety of social relationships.

Herbert, however, does not instruct his parson in these public behaviors simply for the parson's worldly advancement. Like Guazzo, Herbert stresses the connections between "civil conversation" and spiritual growth. Guazzo warns against remaining "mewed up" in solitude and introspection because civil conversation provides a better way for a man to make "a conquest of him selfe."[52] In the same spirit, Herbert recommends social interaction for the parson's own edification. Here, for example, he describes the spiritual benefits of the parson's public teaching: "whereas in Sermons there is a kinde of state, in Catechizing there is an humblenesse very sutable to Christian regeneration, which exceedingly delights [the parson] as by way of exercise upon himself, and by way of preaching to himself, for the advancing of his own mortification; for in preaching to others, he forgets not himself, but is first a Sermon to himself, and then to others; growing with the growth of his Parish (255:9–16).

More than private study or meditation, *The Country Parson* recommends public duties for the parson's own spiritual growth. The parson grows not only as a solitary soul, but "with the growth of his parish."

For the edification of his parish Herbert suggests that the parson's "civil conversation" is invaluable. Other manualists emphasize the primacy of the sermon in teaching the congregation. For Herbert, the parson's public life or "civil conversation" is the best sermon. "The Countrey Parson's . . . holy Life," Herbert writes, "even it selfe is a Sermon" (278:11–14). He further explains: "the Parson having studied, and mastered all his lusts and affections within, and the whole Army of Temptations without, hath ever so many sermons ready penn'd, as he hath victories" (278:24). Of the parson's "conversation" he explains that, upon conquering a particular problem, the parson should relate his method to another: "This Instruction and comfort the parson getting for himself, when he tells it to others, becomes a Sermon" (279:31–33), and again: "For the temptations with which a good man is beset, and the ways which he used to overcome them, being told to another, whether in private conference, or in the Church, are a Sermon" (278:14–18). Even the parson's public disposition is a sermon: "There is much preaching in . . . friendliness" (284:21–22). Herbert makes his point about "civil conversation" in a way which is reminiscent of Guazzo's assertion that civil conversation heals: "And it fares in this as it doth in Physick: He that hath been sick of a Consumption, and knows what recovered him, is a Physitian so far as he meetes with the same disease, and temper; and can much better, and particularly do it, then he that is generally learned, and was never sick. And if the same person had been sick of all diseases, and were recovered of all by things that he knew; there were no such Physician as he, both for skill and tendernesse. Just so it is in Divinity . . . for though the temptations may be diverse in divers Christians, yet the victory is alike in all, being by the self-same Spirit" (278:25–279:2). For Herbert "civil conversation" advances the spiritual health of both pastor and congregation in ways in which mere sermonizing or formal learning cannot.

In addition to the parson's public life and day-to-day discourse for advancing the good of his people, Herbert also values public catechizing. This form of "civil conversation," Herbert explains, "exceeds even Sermons in teaching" (257:20–21). One reason catechizing is so effective is that it aids in self-knowledge. Guazzo writes that civil conversation clothes a man "with knowledge of himselfe,"[53] and that "our judgements, and the knowledge of our selves dependeth on the judgement and conversation of many."[54] In a strikingly similar sense, Herbert describes the "civil conversation" of catechumen and priest as advancing the self-awareness of the student. Here Herbert expresses the superiority of social interaction over the sermon as he describes the "secret" of catechizing: "[Catechizing] is the Practice which the Parson so much commends to all his fellow-labourers; the secret of whose good consists in this, that at Sermons and Prayers men may sleep or wander; but when one is asked a question, he must discover what he is (257:16–20).

This form of "civil conversation" more than sermons or prayers, helps a man "discover what he is." Again, Herbert explains that through public catechizing, the priest's conversationally propounding questions—not merely asking set questions and receiving answers learned by rote, but rather by true conversation (259:6–10)—will help his student to self-awareness. At that point, writes Herbert, "the answerer will discover what hee is" (259:9–10). Herbert emphasizes that "civil conversation" or social interaction "exceeds even Sermons" (257:20) in clothing a man "with the knowledge of himselfe."

Like Guazzo, then, Herbert makes significant spiritual claims for "civil conversation." Public life in *The Country Parson* plays an unusually large role in advancing the religious health and self-knowledge of Herbert's parish.[55] Unlike the typical courtesy authors, both Herbert and Guazzo focus their attention on the outer or public man largely for spiritual ends. Unlike some Puritan authors, Herbert does not hold up the sermon as the best teaching method, but for purposes of education he appears to value at least some kinds of "civil conversation" more. Both Herbert and Guazzo provide strong arguments for the spiritual benefits of man in society.

It is significant that Guazzo also treats in a religious way the relationship between seeming and being. Clearly Guazzo is as interested as any courtesy author in the appearances of the gentleman's outer life and observable behavior. Like Della Casa, Machiavelli, and especially Castiglione, Guazzo devotes a large bulk of his treatise to prescribing just the sort of behavior one should show to particular members of one's community or society. He advises the gentleman on how to act and appear with young men, old men, magistrates, the learned, strangers, women, children, brothers, servants, and so on—Guazzo is interested in the courtier's outward appearances with everyone from the yeoman to the prince. But while the other courtesy authors are most concerned with seeming, Guazzo is just as interested in being. J. L. Lievsay attests to Guazzo's unusual spiritual priorities: "Take moral soundings where you will in Machiavelli, Castiglione, or Della Casa, what you acquire . . . resolves itself to this: It is better *to seem* than *to be.* Take the same soundings in Guazzo, and you will find him ever insistent upon the opposite."[56]

Guazzo is indeed insistent upon the importance of being. Unlike other courtesy authors, he does not recommend cultivating appearances that have no connection to underlying realities. Instead, Guazzo emphasizes that one's appearances should reflect and match one's inner realities. Anniball says a man should "indevour, to bee such a one in deede as hee desireth to seeme to bee in shewe."[57] And again later he reiterates: "a man ought to indevour to bee suche a one, as he desireth to seeme to bee."[58] Guazzo calls for "sinceritie and playne dealing . . . not only in deedes but even in woordes likewise."[59] Guazzo makes his respect for being clear in such statements—which would never be mistaken for Castiglione's or Machiavelli's—as this one: "I am resolute in this, that wee ought to doe well for the love of vertue, and not for the feare of evill report."[60]

But while he insists on the importance of being, Guazzo does not ignore or underestimate the power of appearances. He does not at any time command flatly, "Be what you are," but rather he urges, "Be what you would seem." He appeals, in other words, to what he feels is a quite proper interest in correct appearances. Guazzo assumes that his reader will "seem," and rather than frown on that, he challenges his reader to bring his inner being up to the level of his outward seeming. According to Guazzo, there are in fact appropriate uses of appearances. Seeming can be, for example, an impetus for self-improvement. Guazzo explains: "all those which will be such as they desire to seeme, wil be severe reformers of them selves, and they wil sooner spye their own faultes then others."[61] For Guazzo, seeming is not a way to fool others so much as a way to self-awareness and wholesome self-fashioning. Guazzo is so far from minimizing the importance of appearances as to say that there is something morally unacceptable in intentionally detracting from one's own public image: "in my minde, making your selfe meaner then you are, you offend in a certain abjectnesse of minde, or in a kinde of dissembling. . .I thinke you will not commende those, who having much understanding, stande little or nothing uppon it, or beeing knowen for woorthie men, seeke to imbase themselves by bearing false witnesse against themselves."[62]

Guazzo's concern for appearances, however, extends beyond its significance for the individual. As in his justification for the public life, Guazzo puts forward moral reasons for promoting attention to seeming. One's good outward appearances can actually help others to be good. Guazzo explains how one's commendable "sayings . . . doings . . . and behaviour" can teach others to improve: "so you see many of good judgement, and lesse overseene in themselves, who, without tarying untill they bee reprooved of others, are mooved of their owne proper will, to waygh diligently the sayings, the dooings, and the behaviour of others. And as they learne to eschue those thinges which they see to bee unseemly in any, so they indevour to followe and appropriate to themselves those things which are commendable in others."[63]

Proper seeming, Guazzo suggests, can help others to "properly be." Here he gives an example in instructing the gentleman in reprehending. When one wants to help another by pointing out some fault, the one reprehending must use a "deep discretion" and an "honest kind of deceit": "to use deeper discretion in the matter, wee must use an honest kinde of deceite, and intermingle with the bitternesse of reprehension, the sweetnesse of some prayse. Or wee muste blame others for those faultes whiche are in him whom wee seeke to refourme: or els reprove our selves as subject too suche imperfections. Finally, we ought to reproove our friende in suche sorte, that hee may take it well, and thinke him selfe beeholding too us for it."[64]

Thus one's "seeming" (using "an honest kinde of deceite") can help another to "be" what he ought to be. Guazzo provides examples from public as well as private relationships, as when he instructs court officers on how to appear in order to properly affect the hearts of both the guilty and the innocent: "The last advertisement to bee given to officers in respect of private persons is, that hee shewe himselfe in countenance severe and terrible, which maketh the guiltie afearde, and the guiltlesse bolde, which commonly pleaseth the good, and displeaseth the yll."[65]

In short, Guazzo would have gentlemen use seeming in speech and behavior to "stirre up mens mindes . . . in godlinesse and goodnesse," that is, to help themselves and others be what they ought to be.

We have already discovered the courtesy-like ways in which *The Country Parson* encourages "seeming" in its parson.[66] But Herbert endorses such self-fashioning for reasons quite different from those of the mainstream courtesy authors. Herbert once again takes a position strikingly like Guazzo's and promotes appearances for the purposes of spiritual realities.

The short chapter, "The Parson in mirth," for example, shows how Herbert's parson must sometimes employ seeming for the improvement of others. Here Herbert explains that although the pastor's true temperament is "generally sad," he must occasionally seem pleasant and cheerful in order to more effectively teach and do good to his hearers:

> The Countrey Parson is generally sad, because hee knows nothing but the Crosse of Christ, his mind being defixed on it with those nailes wherewith his Master was: or if he have any leisure

> to look off from thence, he meets continually with two most sad spectacles, Sin, and Misery; God dishonoured every day, and man afflicted. Neverthelesse, he sometimes refresheth himselfe, as knowing that nature will not bear everlasting droopings, and that *pleasantnesse of disposition is a great key to do good*; not onely because all men shun the company of perpetuall severity, but also for that when they are in company, *instructions seasoned with pleasantnesse, both enter sooner, and roote deeper.* Wherefore he condescends to humane frailties . . . and intermingles some mirth in his discourses occasionally, according to the pulse of the hearer. (267:27–268:8, my italics)

Herbert's parson not only alters his own appearances for the good of others, but he also urges his parishioners to "seem in order to be." The parson sees to it—even though his congregation may not in reality be reverent—that they appear so. He suggests that the people's thinking will eventually follow their behavior, or their inner selves will conform to their outer:

> Besides [the parson's] example, he having often instructed his people how to carry themselves in divine service, exacts of them all possible reverence, by no means enduring either talking, or sleeping, or gazing, or leaning, or halfe-kneeling, or any undutiful behaviour in them, but causing them, when they sit, or stand, or kneel, to do all in a strait, and steady posture, *as attending* to what is done in the Church, and every one, man, and child, answering aloud both Amen, and all other answers . . . which answers also are to be done not in a hudling, or slubbering fashion, gaping, or scratching the head, or spitting even in the midst of their answer, but gently and pausably, thinking what they say; so that while they answer . . . they meditate as they speak. (231:20–34, my emphasis)

Here Herbert suggests that by practicing a certain outward behavior, the inner may be changed, as his reluctant parishioners go from the appearance of interest in the service ("as attending to what is done in the church") to true mental engagement ("thinking what they say" and "meditating as they speak"). No other clerical manualist goes into such detail regarding either the parson's or the congregation's behavior. Nor does any other suggest, as Herbert does, that the seeming of the outer man is so important to the being of the inner.

In these ways Herbert agrees with Guazzo's belief that appearances can shape reality. Guazzo states: "I am of the opinion, that a man solemne by nature, may by use get the habite of pleasauntnesse."[67] Even a solemn man, if he *seems* pleasant long enough, will acquire the habit of *being* pleasant. Guazzo further warns that seeming can likewise work in a negative direction. That is, if one shapes his outer man negatively, his inner self will similarly be fashioned: "some of our Citizens, who coveting to bee counted pleasant fellowes, take delight in counterfaiting to speake clownishly, whereof it: commeth to passe, that comming afterwardes into the companie of grave persons, they are not able to refraine those follies, and shewe themselves rusticall, and uncivile in their speach."[68]

Thus while both Herbert and Guazzo, like true courtesy authors, encourage some forms of seeming, they stand out among the rest in their purposes as well as in their confidence that appearances can have a profound mimetic effect upon spiritual realities.

In Herbert's remarkably detailed chapter, "The Parson's Church," (246–47) we find the appearances of the church lovingly described and Herbert's unusual attention to seeming explained.[69] Herbert discusses the "speciall care" the pastor should have for the aesthetic appeal of his building:

> The Countrey Parson hath a speciall care of his Church, that all things there be decent, and befitting his Name by which it is called. Therefore first he takes order, that all things be in good repair; as walls plaistered, windows glazed, floore paved, seats whole, firm, and uniform, especially that the Pulpit, and Desk, and Communion Table, and Font be as they ought, for those great duties that are performed in then. Secondly, that the Church be swept, and kept cleane without dust, or Cobwebs, and at great festivalls strawed, and stuck with boughs, and perfumed with incense. Thirdly, That there be fit, and proper texts of Scripture every where painted, and that all the painting be grave, and reverend, not with light colours, or foolish anticks. Fourthly, That all the books appointed by Authority be there, and those not torne, or fouled, but whole and clean, and well bound; and that there be a fitting, and sightly Communion Cloth of fine linnen, with an handsome, and seemly Carpet of good and costly Stuffe, or Cloth, and all kept sweet and clean, in a strong and decent chest, with a

> Chalice, and Cover, and a Stoop, or Flagon; and a Bason for Almes and offerings; besides which, he hath a Poor-mans Box conveniently seated, to receive the charity of well minded people, and to lay up treasure for the sick and needy. (246:1–22)

Herbert's great concern for the textures, scents, and visual effects of his church suggests an importance for ministerial appearances unparalleled in works of advice to clergy. Following this careful description, Herbert explains this attention to the church's appearances. First Herbert emphasizes that his concern for appearances is not superstitious ("not . . . as putting a holiness in the things"). Yet while Herbert wants to avoid a Roman Catholic veneration of holy things, he will not agree with the "slovenly" ways of those Puritans who seem to care nothing for the appearances of the church and ministry.[70] Thus he counsels a "middle way," which calls for what Herbert believes to be a proper and biblical attention to outer forms.

Next Herbert offers his scriptural apologetic for this "middle way." Quoting 1 Corinthians 14:40, Herbert explains that a proper attention to appearances fulfills St. Paul's injunction to do things "decently and in order," and it likewise glorifies God ("for the honour of God"). Herbert also quotes 1 Corinthians 14:26—"Let all things be done to edification" and suggests that his description in "The Parson's Church" fulfills this injunction. Here we see an affirmation of the role of the senses in spiritual experience, and we see the importance Herbert places upon appearances for the edification or "benefit of our neighbor."[71] Herbert is actually arguing that "walls plaistered, windows glazed, floore paved, seats whole, firm, and uniform," a church "strawed, and stuck with boughs, arid perfumed with incense," and a "Communion Cloth of fine linnen, with an handsome, and seemly Carpet of good and costly stuffe," are important for the faith of believers and not simply external adornment. While Herbert follows tradition in quoting these verses from Corinthians with regard to church practices, he is unique in using them to defend attention to the outer appearances of the church.[72] Like Stefano Guazzo, Herbert argues that right appearances serve to edify.

Herbert gives one final justification for beautifying his church. He explains that while obeying Paul's two rules ("Let all things be done decently and in order" and "let all things be done to edification") by attending to church appearances, the pastor gives witness to the perfection of scripture: "For these two rules comprize and include the double object of our duty, God, and our neighbour; the first being for the honour of God; the second for the benefit of our neighbor. So that they excellently score out the way, and fully, and exactly contain, even in external and indifferent things what course is to be taken; and put them to great shame, who deny the Scripture to be perfect (246:28–247:2).

Herbert does not explain why or how the skeptic is to be put to shame by the parson's attention to "externall and indifferent things." It is clear, however, that Herbert sees a connection between church appearances and apologetics. Somehow the beautiful appearances of a church building argue for the authority of Scripture. Earlier we noted the pastor's external behavior confirming the truth of his doctrine.[73] Now we see that proper appearances in his church can do the same. However Herbert may explain this phenomenon, once again he argues that proper appearances can encourage proper realities. In this instance, creating certain lovely appearances about the church building both edifies the believer and convinces the skeptic.

On the topic of seeming and being then, Guazzo and Herbert depart from their respective genres and share some striking sympathies. The theme of the secular courtesy book is "It is better to seem than to be." The theme of most pastoral manuals is "It is better to be than to seem." Herbert, ostensibly writing a pastoral manual, and Guazzo, ostensibly writing a courtesy book, both modify their respective traditions and assert that artful behavior is useful primarily to change the heart and that proper seeming can generate proper being.

Conclusion

WHEN HERBERT'S *THE COUNTRY PARSON* IS VIEWED AS A COURTESY book for fellow clergymen, the most puzzling aspects of the work become intelligible. Herbert's emphasis on the public side of the parson's life—his manners, clothes, house, furniture, and church building—is appropriate. His aristocratic tone, diction, and subject matter are fitting for a manual designed for courtiers of the Heavenly King. *The Country Parson,* like all courtesy handbooks, offers training for the lives, rather than for the precise doctrines or beliefs of its readers. And according to the best aristocratic conventions of the day, that training is recommended through experience complemented by formal learning, not supplanted by it.

Herbert's techniques for artful, public self-fashioning are similar to those used by all courtesy authors, but his spiritual aims are unusual and demonstrate a remarkable affinity to one writer in particular, Stefano Guazzo. While Guazzo was a sixteenth-century Italian Roman Catholic and Herbert a seventeenth-century English Protestant, they shared a burden for their respective clergymen, which made Guazzo's *The Civile Conversation* fitting inspiration for Herbert's *The Country Parson.*

Guazzo had lamented of the clergy that while they "ought. . . by their good life and doctrine to amend our naughtie lives. . . . Lay men are for the most part of better life and conversation, then spiritual men are."[1] Herbert apparently saw a similar phenomenon in England and therefore decided to depict the duty of a priest, which he explained is "to do that which Christ did and after his manner, both for Doctrine and Life" (225:18–19). Since for both authors it was the life and not the doctrine of the clergy that was questionable, Herbert's focus is on improving his readers' behavior, not their beliefs. Guazzo's unusually pious courtesy manual provided Herbert an ideal model for expressing his thoughts on the contemporary Church of England.

Herbert's eagerness to express his views was undoubtedly piqued by contemporary publications on the ministry. Writings of the Puritan Brotherhood and others threatened to pull English pastorates too far in the direction of the Reformed communion. Herbert's work provides a balance to their decidedly democratic spirit, emphasis on faith, the inner man, and their often skeptical attitude toward appearances. *The Country Parson,* while not denying the importance of a parson's inner life, offers a counterbalancing emphasis on good works, the outer man, and observable forms.

Herbert's obvious love of form, order, and hierarchy might leave the mistaken impression that Herbert's manual was a purely Anglican response to the largely Puritan dominated genre. In fact, Herbert attempted to unite the best of both High and Low Church traditions in the person of his ideal country parson. This is evident in Herbert's mediating choices regarding doctrine, sermon style, exegesis, and ceremonial accouterments. It is also expressed in his emphasis on the sanctification of the minister, good works, and appearances as opposed to stressing the minister's salvation, preaching, and conversion. As in his poem, "The British Church," Herbert expresses in *The Country Parson* the ideal as the *via media* between Roman Catholic "superstition" and Reformed "slovenliness." But the subject of appearances, a metaphor for doctrine and practice in "The British Church," becomes a central issue in *The County Parson.* The ideal country parson is neither superstitious about the occult powers of appearances as in gestures, garments, or other "holy" things associated with the priesthood; nor is he reluctant to manipulate appearances to his particular ends. His parson creates an aura of beauty, grace, and holiness and thus avoids the "slovenliness" Herbert perceives to be the error of some Protestant sects.

Like all courtesy authors, Herbert shapes appearances to win the love and favor of his observers. But like Stefano Guazzo alone, Herbert recommends using appearances, not for the self-advancement of the "courtier," but for the true spiritual good of others. Many of Herbert's contemporary divines deplored the poor example of the "loose livers" among the clergy. But while most manualists called for soul-searching, repentance, and conversion, Herbert called for a beautifying of one's life. He does so for two reasons: first, Herbert holds an exalted view of the Church of England. He believes that one's duties toward God can be fulfilled by properly performing one's obligations within the Church. He sees no need for urging conversion on the clergy because he apparently believes that the priest who sincerely participates in the rites of the Church is, by the proof of that participation, a truly converted man. Herbert focuses then on the clergy's sanctification, not justification. Herbert, again like Guazzo, also believes in the mimetic power of appearances. That is, he maintains that if inner realities are not as they should be, shaping the outer man is one way to effect the desired internal change. In other words, inner spiritual realities often follow the lead of outer actions. Both Herbert and Guazzo show that artful appearances can be used to transform one's inner self as well as the inner selves of others. This is how Herbert can make such striking claims as he does in "The Parson's Church," where he holds that a beautiful and orderly church building will convince the skeptic of the veracity of the scripture,[2] or as in "The Parson arguing," where Herbert asserts that the heretic will be converted to the faith by the beauty of the parson's life.[3]

This consideration of appearances in *The Country Parson* may he useful to students of Herbert's poetry. For example, it might be applied to a reading of the first poem in *The Temple*, "The Church Porch." The criticism on this piece is often apologetic because the seemingly superficial nature of the poem makes it sound trite and out of place among the authentic, personal, and passionate poems of *The Temple*. Every reader of *The Temple* is aware of its intimate voice and spiritual depths. What then do we make of the opening poem in which Herbert sounds so superficial and uninspired? Here he moralistically warns against drunkenness, lying, idleness, boasting, gaming, and debt. He instructs youth on proper dressing, polite conversation, friendship, disposition, and even how to laugh. These overtly didactic instructions on manners stand in strange contrast to the profoundly spiritual poetry that makes up the rest of *The Temple*.

Rather than a lapse in Herbert's powers, "The Church Porch" is an introduction very much in keeping with Herbert's pastoral and poetic strategies for reaching the heart. "The Church Porch" deals, in fact, with many of those same topics covered in contemporary courtesy books. At one point Herbert even uses an injunction from his own "courtesy book." In *The Country Parson* Herbert instructs one to dress so as to suggest the cleanliness of one's mind: "The Parsons . . . apparrell [is] plaine, but reverend, and clean, without spots, or dust, or smell; the purity of his mind breaking out, and dilating it self even to his body, clothes and habitation" (228:10–13). "The Church Porch" likewise instructs: "Let thy mindes sweetnesse have his operation / Upon thy body, clothes, and habitation" (21:371–72).

Preparation for the inward walk through "The Church" must begin with attention to the outer man. After "The Church Porch" and before "The Church," in what Herbert calls the "Superliminare," he therefore writes:

> Thou, whom the former precepts have
> Sprinkled and taught, how to behave
> Thy self in church; approach, and taste
> The Churches mystical repast.
>
> (25:1–4)

Just as *The Country Parson* gives instructions for the behavior of priest and people, "The Church Porch" prepares the reader for a significant spiritual experience not by directly addressing the heart, but by encouraging the outer man to a posture of reverence. The inner man is expected to follow. That Herbert should choose to introduce his intensely inward volume of poems with a "how to" on manners and courteous behavior is less puzzling when studied in light of *The Country Parson*. "The Church Porch" is to *The Temple* what *The Country Parson* is to the ministry, a preparatory "courtesy book" that will allow true "heart work and heaven work," in Richard Baxter's phrase, to go forward.

Understanding the function of *The Country Parson* also may help to unite two sides of a long-standing schism in Herbert criticism. Since Rosemond Tuve's landmark work, *A Reading of George Herbert*, appeared in 1952, critics have been divided over the best method for approaching Herbert's poetry. Roughly speaking, Herbert's work might be said to be treated either primarily as a religious phenomenon or primarily as a technical or artistic achievement. Some, following Rosemond Tuve, (i.e., Joseph Summers, Louis Martz, Barbara Lewalski, and others) enhanced our understanding of Herbert by elucidating Herbert's debts and contributions to a spiritual tradition.[4] Their methods are largely historical and their conclusions often theological. They follow Rosemond Tuve who saw the key to understanding Herbert (and those she categorized as other authors of "metaphysical poems") in his religious "reading of life" more than in his technique. "We need to ask of a metaphysical poem," Tuve writes, "how its metaphors operate to provide insight and not what peculiar tricks of technique and modernities of temper it exhibits. The way a poem is written inescapably constitutes some thinking mind's reading of life, and the secret of metaphysical wit lies in a reading of life (of the nature of truth and of knowledge) inherited through at least the ten or twelve preceding centuries."[5]

Placing Herbert's poetry within a "reading of life . . . inherited through at least the ten or twelve preceding centuries" contrasts sharply with the methods of other Herbert scholars like Helen Vendler, Mary Ellen Rickey, Arnold Stein, and Stanley Fish. They find Herbert's aesthetic rather than his religious insight his crowning achievement. Arnold Stein in his *George Herbert's Lyrics* speaks for his colleagues when he calls the reader "ignorant" who cannot admire the techniques of Herbert's lyrics "immediately for their own sake."[6] In his final chapter Stein addresses the problem of the religious poem in which style is always threatened by prior religious commitment. The religious poet must somehow refuse to be "cramped" in his art by these commitments: "The common danger is that the significant form will be narrowly ordered, with a free discovery of individual rightness cramped by prior obligations. . . ."[7] Through various examples from *The Temple* Stein shows Herbert to have avoided such "cramping" by conscientious attention to poetic form: "Herbert's characteristic solutions are not independently determined by his religious beliefs and . . . his attitudes toward poetic form are deeply involved in all the poetic decisions he makes."[8] Stein sums up the aesthetic focus of this kind of criticism with the brief observation: "What is said in a poem must be judged by what is done in that poem."[9]

In *The Living Temple* by Stanley Fish, the issue is raised and expanded. Fish characterizes the problem this way: our understanding of Herbert's sincerity as a religious thinker often collides with our perception of him as an artist. The critic is therefore "constrained to choose between de-emphasizing the one or domesticating the other."[10] In deciding an approach to Herbert's poetry the scholar may tacitly respond to this question: "Are Herbert's poems really an almost miraculous transcription of a genuine interior phenomenon, or is he a poet first, making creative use of spiritual material—perhaps personally experienced, perhaps not?"[11] If the critic sees Herbert above all as a religious figure, *The Temple* might be seen as a series of accurate reflections of a "thinking mind's reading of life," and examining this reading becomes the focus of the criticism. Such a critic's work will be dominated by Herbert's use of religious traditions, his spiritual insights and dramas. If, however, the scholar perceives Herbert as first and foremost an artist, there is a sense in which Herbert's personal religious experience becomes subordinate to the poet's creative process. Such a reader will de-emphasize any spiritual and biographical essence in the poems to focus on Herbert's technical success.

Is there a way to evaluate Herbert as an artist without undermining the authenticity of his religious expression? Our study of *The Country Parson* may provide a useful model. If Herbert in fact believed in the efficacy of appearances and the power of the observable to shape the unobservable, his creative process—and his religious experience as well—may need to be viewed another way. Rather than imagining Herbert as either transcribing a past spiritual experience into poetry or as imagining him as merely using religious materials for a higher aesthetic end, perhaps we ought to conceive of Herbert as first shaping poetic and religious forms, which then create corresponding experiences. That is, instead of thinking of Herbert's poems as records of past thoughts or events, we might think of the poems as actual precursors or catalysts to spiritual events, insights, or dramas. In the process of writing "The Collar," for example, Herbert may have encountered his own feelings of rebellion and submission in an authentic manner not fully possible without actually writing a poem. In a phenomenon experienced by others, Herbert's attentiveness to religious and aesthetic forms may have inspired internal responses of corresponding significance and beauty.[12]

What Herbert recommends in *The Country Parson* then becomes analogous to his own act of writing poetry. In *The Country Parson* Herbert seeks to develop the spiritual life of both parson and people by first shaping their outer forms and behavior—hopeful, even confident that the essence will follow. Through the act of writing *The Temple* Herbert may have clarified interior experiences that corresponded to the poetic images of spiritual wrestling, insights, resolutions, and celebrations we find in *The Temple*. That is, Herbert's authentic inner realities may have been shaped, developed, and finally fully realized through the creative process of writing. Herbert builds his temple, we might say, before he dwells in it. And he invites others to join him there.

As with *The Country Parson*, a reader may experience the unexpected mimesis of his own heart conforming itself to the image of the spiritual life he finds in *The Temple*. This is surely Herbert's intent. In the dedication to *The Temple* he hopes that those would "turn their eyes hither who shall make gain" (5). If *The Temple* then is a spiritual model, it is the private side of the public man Herbert calls the Country Parson. This parson is an example of what all priests ought to be. But the Country Parson is only an artifact unless—as Herbert expresses his hope in his poem "Obedience"—someone will "Thrust his heart" (105:42) into the work. Taken together, *The Country Parson* and *The Temple* then may constitute a single work of art, which Herbert, Pygmalion-like, prayed would come to life.

Notes

Introduction

1. Most of Herbert's literary critics show interest in *The Country Parson* for a word or phrase supporting a reading for a particular poem in *The Temple*. Other critics, Louis Martz, for example, and Barbara Lewalski, enlist parts of *The Country Parson* toward broader conclusions regarding the entire seventeenth century. Stanley Fish in *The Living Temple: George Herbert and Catechizing* briefly considers a chapter from *The Country Parson* in the service of a reading for *The Temple*. Joseph Summers examines *The Country Parson* in several pages of *George Herbert: His Religion and Art* in relation to Herbert's use of language. Richard Strier in *Love Known* makes considerable reference to *The Country Parson*, but always in the service of his interests in *The Temple*. Michael Schoenfeldt makes copious references to *The Country Parson* to support his thesis in *Prayer and Power: George Herbert and Renaissance Courtship*, as does Christopher Hodgkins in *Authority, Church and Society in George Herbert: Return to the Middle Way*. Biographers Margaret Bottrall, Amy Charles, and Cristina Malcolmson (in *George Herbert* and *A Life of George Herbert* and *George Herbert: A Literary Life*, respectively) devote considerable space to *The Country Parson* for historical purposes.

2. Articles exclusively devoted to *The Country Parson* include Harold H. Kollmeier, "*The Country Parson* in Its Time"; Daniel Doerksen, "'Too Good for Those Times': Politics and the Publication of George Herbert's *The Country Parson*"; Douglas J. Swartz, *"Discourse and Direction: A Priest to the Temple, or, The Country Parson* and the Elaboration of Sovereign Rule"; and Cristina Malcolmson, "George Herbert's *The Country Parson* and the Character of Social Identity." The only published book dedicated to *The Country Parson* is Ronald W. Cooley's *'Full of all knowledg': George Herbert's* Country Parson *and Early Modern Social Discourse,* which is primarily a sociological study, placing *The Country Parson* in its cultural milieu and illuminating contemporary practices in agriculture, professional, social, and domestic affairs.

Two literary analyses of *The Country Parson* (written by this author) are reproduced in enlarged forms here: "All Possible Art: George Herbert's *The Country Parson* and Courtesy" first appeared in *The John Donne Journal,* Volume 8. With some revision, it makes up chapter 3 of this study. A second publication largely overlaps with chapter 4: "George Herbert's *The Country Parson* and

Stefano Guazzo's *The Civile Conversation*" has recently appeared in the *George Herbert Journal* 27, nos. 1 and 2.

3. C. A. Patrides, ed., *The English Poems of George Herbert* (London: Dent, 1974), 11.

4. M. M. Mahood, *Poetry and Humanism* (1949; repr., New York: Norton, 1970), 41.

5. Marion White Singleton, *God's Courtier: Configuring a Different Grace in George Herbert's Temple* (Cambridge: Cambridge University Press, 1987), 7.

6. Michael C. Schoenfeldt, *Prayer and Power: George Herbert and Renaissance Courtship* (Chicago: University of Chicago Press, 1991), 5.

7. Ronald W. Cooley, *'Full of all knowledg': George Herbert's* Country Parson *and Early Modern Social Discourse* (Toronto: University of Toronto Press, 2004), 36.

8. Cristina Malcolmson, *George Herbert: A Literary Life* (New York: Palgrave Macmillan, 2004), 112.

9. *The Works of George Herbert*, ed. F. E. Hutchinson (Oxford: Clarendon Press, 1941), 232. Used by permission of Oxford University Press. Hereafter all quotations from Herbert will be from this edition and will be cited in the text by page and line number.

Chapter 1. Doctrine and Life

1. Helen Vendler, *The Poetry of George Herbert* (Cambridge, MA: Harvard University Press, 1975), 79.

2. Vendler, *Poetry of George Herbert*, 80.

3. This is not to suggest that Herbert held a low view of the importance of doctrine for the church or the believer. I quite agree with Daniel W. Doerksen that, for Donne and Herbert and their contemporaries, "Doctrine was . . . regarded as foundational to the church, really of the essence." *Conforming to the Word: Herbert, Donne, and the English Church before Laud* (Lewisburg: Bucknell University Press, 1997), 71. But the unusual treatment of doctrine in *The Country Parson* calls for a closer examination and explanation, as this study hopes to provide.

4. Barbara Kiefer Lewalski, *Protestant Poetics and the Seventeenth-Century Religious Lyric* (Princeton, NJ: Princeton University Press, 1968), 15–18.

5. Richard Baxter, *The Reformed Pastor* (1656; New York: The American Tract Society, 1829), 72. Used here and hereafter by permission of the American Tract Society, Garland, Texas.

6. William Ames, *The Marrow of Theology*, trans. and ed. John D. Eusden (1629; Boston: Pilgrim Press, 1968), 79–80.

7. All biblical quotations taken from *The Authorized Version of the English Bible* (1611) unless otherwise indicated.

8. John Calvin, *Calvin's New Testament Commentaries*, eds. David W. Torrance and Thomas F. Torrance, vols. 1–12 (Grand Rapids, MI: Eerdmans, 1964), 10:191.

9. James Gardiner, *Advice to the Clergy of the Diocese of Lincoln* (London: The Star in Ludgate-Street, 1697), 9.

10. Baxter, *Reformed Pastor*, 89.

11. Ronald Cooley has made similar observations: "the ideal parson depicted in the chapters is a fabric of precepts for external behaviour," and "As any chapter in *The Country Parson* will testify, Herbert differs from both Donne and Hooker in stressing the importance of 'an exemplar life'." Ronald Cooley, *'Full of all knowledg': George Herbert's* Country Parson *and Early Modern Social Discourse* (Toronto: University of Toronto Press, 2003), 22, 51.

12. Conspicuous for its absence is Herbert's silence on the pastor's own spirituality. Barbara Lewalski describes the more typical Protestant preparation for sermons: "indeed Protestants generally agreed that worthy sermons and prayers must spring from inner illumination by the Spirit, and from the experience of grace and redemption: whatever the role of art, the artist and his matter must first be formed by God." Lewalski, *Protestant Poetics*, 216.

13 Others have pointed out the affinities between *The Country Parson* and character books (for example Alfred Ainger, H. C. Beeching, Eliz. Clarke, and Elbert Thompson). Note how the title page to *The Country Parson* appears:

A PRIEST to the TEMPLE
or
The Country Parson
HIS
CHARACTER
AND
Rule of Holy Life

"Character" here receives special attention, which may have been Herbert's intention. Notice further that nearly every chapter begins, "The Country Parson . . . " after the form of character books; see Overbury's or Earle's characters, for example. Each sketch begins in this form: "The Good Wife . . . " or "The Child . . . " and so on.

14. Joseph Summers, *George Herbert: His Religion and Art* (Cambridge, MA: Harvard University Press, 1954), 101.

15. Gilbert Burnet, *A Discourse of the Pastoral Care* (1692; London: Rivingtons and Cochran, 1821), 101.

16. See also Matt. 6:2–6; 23:1–12; Luke 18:10–14.

17. Even here Herbert gauges spiritual life by a person's life rather than his doctrine, what he does rather than what he believes.

18. Martin Luther, *Luther's Works*, eds. Hilton C. Oswald and Jaroslav Pelikan, vols. 1–30 (St. Louis, MO: Concordia Publishing House, 1972), 28:228.

19. Calvin, *New Testament Commentaries*, 10:385 (my italics).

20. Baxter, *Reformed Pastor*, 145.

21. Barbara Lewalski in *Protestant Poetics* quotes Henry R. McAdoo saying, "Calvinism . . . was in the ascendant in England until the middle of the [17th] century. The disagreement between Anglican and Puritan began with questions of church order and not of teaching, and it has been said that there was hardly one of the Elizabethan bishops who was not a Calvinist"—Lewalski, 13. See also Charles D. Cremeans, *The Reception of Calvinistic Thought in England* (Urbana: University of Illinois Press, 1949).

22. Luther, *Works*, 23:75.

23. Calvin, *New Testament Commentaries,* 12:233.

24. William Beveridge, *Ecclesia Anglicana Ecclesia Catholica OR The Doctrine of the Church of England Consonant To Scripture, Reason, and Fathers: in a Discourse upon the Thirty Nine Articles Agreed Upon in the Convocation Held At London, MDLXII* (Oxford: Oxford University Press, 1847), 343.

25. This is not to say that Herbert disagreed with his church's teaching on predestination. Daniel Doerksen writes: "Herbert knew that his church had a strong, positive position on the topic of predestination, and he shared in it." *Conforming to the Word*, 79. Nevertheless, Herbert's strong emphasis on behavior in *The Country Parson* suggests a specific agenda for the work, which this study hopes to investigate.

26. Amy Charles, *A Life of George Herbert* (Ithaca, NY: Cornell University Press, 1977), 51.

27. *Parallel New Testament in Greek and English*, (Grand Rapids, MI: Zondervan Bible Publishers, 1975).

28. Luther, *Works*, 23:229.

29. Calvin, *New Testament Commentaries,* 4:185.

30. Ibid., 4:221–22.

31. Beveridge, *Ecclesia Anglicana*, 308.

32. One may postulate that another explanation for Herbert's emphasis on the outer man in *The Country Parson* is that here he is speaking in a "pastoral persona," quite distinct from the poetic persona of *The Temple*. In his poetry, Herbert had already treated the subject of the inner man to a striking degree of depth and intimacy. As Herbert is said to have put it to his friend, Ferrar, his poems reflected "the many spiritual Conflicts that have past betwixt God and my Soul" (Hutchinson, xxxvii).

Chapter 2. Contemporary Clerical Manuals

1. Ilona Bell, "Setting Foot into Divinity: George Herbert and the English Reformation," *Modern Language Quarterly* 38 (1977): 220–21.

2. Joseph Summers, *George Herbert: His Religion and Art* (Cambridge, MA: Harvard University Press, 1954), 13.

3. Richard Baxter, *Preface to Poetical Fragments* (London, 1681), quoted in Hutchinson, *Works of George Herbert*, xliv. Used by permission of Oxford University Press.

4. The terms "High Church" or "Anglo-Catholic" and "Puritan" or "Reformed" have often been oversimplified, and consequently misunderstood. Gene Edward Veith's essay, "The Religious Wars in George Herbert Criticism: Reinterpreting Seventeenth-Century Anglicanism" *George Herbert Journal* 11, no. 2 (1988), points out the most common misconceptions associated with these labels. He concludes that to speak accurately, Herbert should be described as "a high church Calvinist Episcopalian" (29). Despite the inherent imprecision of the terms, it is still necessary for our discussion to distinguish important factions within the church of Herbert's time (as Herbert himself did in "The British Church"). I will use the familiar terms "Anglo-Catholic" and "Puritan," in their

broadly understood meanings, fully aware that these conventional models are more complex and overlapping than they have often been understood.

5. Rosemond Tuve, *A Reading of George Herbert* (London: Faber and Faber, 1952); Louis L. Martz, *The Poetry of Meditation* (New Haven, CT: Yale University Press, 1962); Stanley Stewart, *George Herbert* (Boston: Twayne Publishers, 1986); William H. Halewood: *The Poetry of Grace: Reformation Themes And Structures in English Seventeenth-Century Poetry* (New Haven, CT: Yale University Press, 1970); Joseph H. Summers, *George Herbert: His Religion and Art* (Cambridge, MA: Harvard University Press, 1954); Richard Strier, *Love Known: Theology and Experience in George Herbert's Poetry* (Chicago: University of Chicago Press, 1983); Barbara Kiefer Lewalski, *Protestant Poetics and the Seventeenth-Century Religious Lyric* (Princeton, NJ: Princeton University Press, 1968).

6. Bell, "*Setting Foot Into Divinity*," 219–41.

7. Amy Charles makes the same point from "The Parson in Sacraments." She argues that while Herbert had "caught the spirit" of Laudian reforms as a student at Cambridge, he "quietly and skillfully" declares an end to partisan bickering over the posture appropriate for communion by writing: "Contentiousnesse in a feast of Charity is more scandal than any posture." Amy Charles, *A Life of George Herbert* (Ithaca, NY: Cornell University Press, 1977), 233.

8. Herbert's thought coincides exactly with the "middle way" chosen by the framers of the Thirty-nine Articles: "The church hath power to decree rights of ceremonies and authority in matters of faith. And yet it is not lawful for the church to ordain anything that is contrary to God's word written"—Article 20.

9. William Perkins, *The works of that famous and worthy minister of Christ.* (London: John Legatt, 1631) 2:222.

10. Charles H. and Katherine George, *The Protestant Mind of the English Reformation, 1570–1640* (Princeton, NJ: Princeton University Press, 1961), 338.

11. W. Fraser Mitchell, *English Pulpit Oratory from Andrewes to Tillotson* (New York: Russell & Russell, 1962), 362.

12. Perry Miller, *The New England Mind: The Seventeenth Century* (New York: Macmillan, 1939), 332.

13. Ibid., 244.

14. Ibid., 333.

15. William Haller, *The Rise of Puritanism* (New York: Columbia University Press, 1938), 180.

16. William Perkins, *Of the Calling of the Ministrie,* 2 parts (London, 1605).

17. Richard Bernard, *The Faithfull Shepheard: Or the Shepheards Faithfulnesse* (London, 1607).

18. *Dictionary of National Biography*, (Oxford: Oxford University Press, 1917), 15:892–95.

19. Ibid., 15:893.

20. Ibid., 2:386.

21. Ibid., 15:894.

22. See Haller, *Rise of Puritanism*, 52–54 and David D. Hall, *The Faithfull Shepherd: A History of the New England Ministry in the Seventeenth Century* (Chapel Hill: University of North Carolina Press, 1972), 48ff.

23. Thomas Hooker in Hall, *Faithfull Shepherd*, 50.
24. Ibid., 50.
25. Perkins, *Of the Calling,* 1:16.
26. Ibid., 1:14–15.
27. Richard Baxter, *The Reformed Pastor* (1656; New York: The American Tract Society, 1829), 89. Used by permission of the American Tract Society, Garland, Texas.
28. Ibid., 90.
29. J. Sears McGee, *The Godly Man in Stuart England: Anglicans, Puritans, and the Two Tables, 1620–1670* (New Haven, CT: Yale University Press, 1976), ix.
30. Ibid., 60.
31. Quoted in McGee, *Godly Man*, 60.
32. Baxter, *Reformed Pastor*, 101.
33. Ibid., 290.
34. Perkins, *Of the Calling*, 2:114.
35. Gilbert Burnet, *A Discourse of the Pastoral Care* (1692; London: Rivington's and Cochran, 1821), 248.
36. Perkins, *Of the Calling,* 1:35.
37. Burnet, *Pastoral Care*, 203.
38. Baxter, *Reformed Pastor*, 116.
39. Herbert could urge pastors to "do that which Christ did" because like most Anglicans he was confident of the Christian's ability to imitate Christ to a significant degree. Puritans, with their heightened awareness of man's depravity, were less confident of the possibility of mimesis: "Anglican divines frequently recommended that Christians use Christ as an exemplar for human behavior . . . Puritans, on the other hand, spoke a great deal of the importance of "possessing" Christ or having an "interest" or "portion" in him, but they rarely suggested the use of Christ's actions as a model . . . The puritan relationship with Christ was often intimate, but seldom imitative." McGee, *Godly Man*, 107. In his recommendation to imitate Christ, Herbert was once again distinguishing himself from his Puritan colleagues.
40. McGee, *Godly Man*, ix.
41. Ibid., 93.
42. Ibid., 94.
43. Ibid., 94.
44. Ibid., 95.
45. Quoted in McGee, *Godly Man*, 64.
46. Baxter, *Reformed Pastor*, 144.
47. Ibid., 144–145.
48. Bernard, *Faithfull Shepheard*, 6.
49. Burnet, *Pastoral Care*, 136.
50. Perkins, *Of the Calling*, 2:75.
51. Ibid., 2:8.
52. Ibid., 1:30.
53. Ibid., 1:49.
54. Ibid., 2:24.

55. Bernard, *Faithfull Shepheard*, 1.
56. Ibid., 2.
57. William Ames. *The Marrow of Theology*. trans. and ed. by John D. Eusden (1629; Boston, MA: Pilgrim Press, 1968), 191.
58. Because Anglicans had less anxiety about conversion, they focused their attention on good works instead. "Puritans had been accused of boiling down all religion to the ear, but Anglicans could equally be accused of contracting it to the hand." McGee, *Godly Man*, 106.
59. Miller, *New England Mind*, 352.
60. Ibid.
61. Bernard, *Faithfull Shepheard*, A3.
62. Ibid., 35–42.
63. Ibid., 36–37.
64. Ibid., 42.
65. Perkins, *Of the Calling*, 1:11.
66. Ibid., 1:11.
67. Ibid., 1:13.
68. Ibid., 1:13–14.
69. McGee, *Godly Man*, 97.
70. In chapter 1 we noted that Herbert writes precious little on text expostulation—three sentences—but instead devotes nearly the whole chapter to pulpit appearances and sermon delivery.
71. See chapter 1.
72. Bernard, *Faithfull Shepheard*, 94.
73. Chapters 3 and 4 of this study will take up this discussion.
74. This is not to identify all Puritans with those who (like some Anabaptists and other more radical Protestants) would advocate extemporaneous preaching. Most Puritans highly valued learning and insisted on scholarly sermon preparation. The point here is that while Puritans encouraged great attention to the preparation of the sermon text, Herbert's focus is on sermon delivery.
75. Burnet, *Pastoral Care*, 187.
76. Ibid., 186–187.
77. Baxter, *Reformed Pastor*, 353.
78. Bernard, *Faithfull Shepheard*, 88.
79. Ames, *Marrow of Theology*, 195.
80. Ibid., 194.
81. Bernard, *Faithfull Shepheard*, 12–13.
82. Perkins, *Of the Calling*, 1:6.
83. Baxter, *Reformed Pastor*, 216.
84. Ibid., 129.

Chapter 3. The Courtesy Tradition

1. William Perkins, *Of the Calling of the Ministrie,* 2 parts (London, 1605).
2. John Jackson, *Ecclesiastes. The Worthy Church-man* (London: R. More, 1628).

3. Richard Baxter, *The Reformed Pastor* (1656; New York: The American Tract Society, 1829), 72. Used by permission of The American Tract Society, Garland, Texas.

4. For example, Perkins's *Of the Calling of the Ministrie* and Jackson's *The Worthy Church-man* provide excellent examples of this method.

5. Baxter begins "Reverend and Dear Brethren, our business here this day is to humble our souls before the Lord." *The Reformed Pastor,* 199.

6. See for example the final paragraph of Bernard's *The Faithfull Shepheard* (London, 1607) or Perkins's *Of the Calling of the Ministrie.*

7. *The Country Parson* thus stands well outside of the growing trend in seventeenth-century England noted by Gertrude Noyes: "A surprising but quite common occurrence is the merging of the sermon and the courtesy book into a curiously amphibious product." Gertrude E. Noyes, *Bibliography of Courtesy and Conduct Books in Seventeenth-Century England* (New Haven, CT: The Tuttle, Morehouse & Taylor Co., 1937), 8.

8. In this regard the Anglican Herbert and the Puritan manualists fall nicely into Joan Webber's rubric for seventeenth-century prose style. Of the Puritans she generalizes: "None of them is thinking of what he does in terms of art, but primarily in terms of practicality–what it will accomplish." The Anglican, she argues, is more interested in an artful manipulation of prose: "the Anglican delights in stylistic complications, and even in playful and recreative devices. Readers are at least implicitly invited to share in the literary life of the book." *The Eloquent "I"* (Madison: University of Wisconsin Press, 1968), 251–52.

9. See the introduction to this work for a summary of the scholarship on this topic.

10. Michael C. Schoenfeldt, *Prayer and Power: George Herbert and Renaissance Courtship* (Chicago: University of Chicago Press, 1991), 272.

11. Henry Peacham, *Peacham's Compleat Gentleman* (1634; Oxford: Clarendon Press, 1906), 223.

12. While many divines describe all depraved men as "led more by sense than faith," Herbert shows his class consciousness by particularly characterizing the country laborer this way.

13. About the period's other conduct books Gertrude Noyes observes that "here the historian and the sociologist may watch the new forces of Puritanism, commercialism, and democracy as they touch the daily lives of the people." Noyes, *Bibliography of Courtesy and Conduct Books*, 2.

14. Ruth Kelso, *The Doctrine of the English Gentleman in the Sixteenth Century* (Gloucester, MA: Peter Smith, 1964), 88. Used by permission of Peter Smith Publishers.

15. Stefano Guazzo, *The Civile Conversation of M. Steven Guazzo*, trans. George Pettie (1581) and Bartholomew Young (1586), ed. Edward Sullivan, 2 vols. (New York: Alfred A. Knopf, 1925), 2, 52.

16. Richard Brathwaite, *The English Gentleman* (1630; London: John Dawson, 1941).

17. English Courtesy authors especially inveighed against idleness. See Elbert N. S. Thompson *Literary Bypaths of the Renaissance* (New Haven, CT:

Yale University Press, 1924), 153, and Lewis B. Wright *Middle-Class Culture in Elizabethan England* (Chapel Hill: University of North Carolina Press, 1935), 127.

18. Though he does not specifically mention the ministry for younger sons of noble men, Herbert's own choice of the church as a profession can surely be seen as an example to inspire others.

19. On this point it is interesting to note that Herbert chose to translate into English *A Treatise of Temperance and Sobrietie* by Lud. Cornarus (Hutchinson, 291–303). Used by permission of Oxford University Press.

20. Baldesar Castiglione, *The Book of the Courtier*, Illus., ed. Edgar Mayhew, © 1959 by Charles S. Singleton and Edgar Mayhew, trans. Charles S. Singleton (New York: Doubleday, 1959), 293. Used by permission of Doubleday, a division of Random House, Inc.

21. Guazzo, *Civile Conversation*, 1:155.

22. To the conventional four he adds two more, which he calls "majesty" and "humanity."

23. Peacham, *Compleat Gentleman*, 4 ff.

24. Kelso, *English Gentleman*, 76.

25. Ibid., 74.

26. Ibid., 72.

27. Ibid., 73.

28. Among the courtly virtues, justice was clearly held to be the chief. Sir Thomas Elyot writes of justice that "without it none other virtue may be commendable, nor . . . any manner of doctrine profitable." Thomas Elyot. *The Book Named the Governor.* ed. S. E. Lehmberg (1531; London: Dent, 1962), 159. It is significant, then, to observe Herbert's exaltation of justice. When he declares, "And justice is the ground of Charity" (262:17–18), he suggests that the cardinal classical virtue, justice, is somehow prior to the cardinal Christian virtue, charity.

29. Perkins writes: "the minister may, yea and must privately use at his libertie the arts, Philosophy, and a variety of reading whilest he is in framing his sermon: but he ought in publicke to conceale all these from the people, and not make the least ostentation." Quoted in W. Fraser Mitchell, *English Pulpit Oratory* (New York: Russell & Russell, 1962), 100.

30. William Haller, *The Rise of Puritanism* (New York: Columbia University Press, 1938), 268.

31. Haller, *Rise of Puritanism*, 267–68.

32. See chapters 1 and 2.

33. It is significant that Herbert discusses such extrabiblical topics like courtesy and liberality. The word "courtesy" does not even appear in the 1611 Authorized Version of the Bible and "liberality" appears only twice.

34. Quoted in Kelso, *English Gentleman*, 88–89.

35. Castiglione, *Courtier*, 316–17, (my emphasis).

36. Niccolò Machiavelli, *The Prince*, trans. and ed. Robert M. Adams (New York: Norton, 1977), 28, 65-66 (my emphasis). Although in his chapter "On Liberality and Stinginess" Machiavelli explains that it is best for the prince to be known as a miser among the common people (showing liberality to everyone

has an enormous cost), he instructs the prince to court his courtiers and army with liberality.

37. Guazzo, *Civile Conversation*, 1:18.

38. Kelso, *English Gentleman*, 89.

39. Ibid., 89.

40. Machiavelli, *Prince*, 68.

41. Castiglione, *Courtier*, 320.

42. Elyot, *Governor*, 102.

43. Thomas Watson, *A Body of Practical Divinity* (London: Bible & Three Crowns, 1686), 174.

44. Watson, *Practical Divinity*, 176.

45. Ibid., 174–77.

46. Kelso, *English Gentleman*, 87.

47. Guazzo, *Civile Conversation*, 1:168 (my emphasis).

48. Quoted in Kelso, *English Gentleman*, 81 (my emphasis).

49. Giovanni Della Casa, *Galateo: Of Manners and Behaviours*, ed. Lewis Einstein (Boston: The Merrymount Press, 1914), 14–15.

50. Guazzo, *Civile Conversation*, 1:166, 194, 192.

51. Castiglione, *Courtier*, 96.

52. Ibid., 11 (my emphasis).

53. Guazzo, *Civile Conversation*, 1:208.

54. Castiglione, *Courtier*, 319.

55. Machiavelli, *Prince*, 52.

56. Elyot, *Governor*, 107.

57. Peacham, *Compleat Gentleman*, 224.

58. Castiglione, *Courtier*, 294.

59. See chapter 2.

60. Guazzo, *Civile Conversation*, 1:158.

61. The Puritans also studied the rhetorical arts in order to better communicate their message. But while the Puritan "esteemed that preaching best wherein was most of God, least of man," Herbert was not reluctant to intermingle with the holy text "Profane utterances of men" (stories, proverbs, and sayings)—Mitchell, *English Pulpit Oratory*, 100. Nor was Herbert hesitant to use the "pagan" methods of liberality and courtesy to "make his higher purposes slip the more easily" (249: 11–12).

62. See chapter 1.

63. See chapter 2.

64. Kelso, *English Gentleman*, 119.

65. Castiglione, *Courtier*, 67.

66. Ibid., 68 (my emphasis).

67. Castiglione, *Courtier*, 70.

68. Ibid., 70–71.

69. Ibid., 71.

70. Quoted in Kelso, *English Gentleman*, 125.

71. Peacham, *Compleat Gentleman*, 2.

72. The great Renaissance courtier and defender of letters, Sir Philip Sidney wrote: "the ending end of all earthly learning" is "virtuous action." —*A Defense of Poetry*, ed. J. S. Van Dorsten (Oxford: Oxford University Press, 1966), 29.

73. Kelso, *English Gentleman*, 126.
74. See Castiglione, *Courtier*.
75. See Peacham, *Compleat Gentleman*.
76. See Elyot, *Governor*.
77. James Cleland, *The Institution of a Young Nobleman*. (1607; New York: Scholars' Facsimiles & Reprints, 1948).
78. Castiglione, *Courtier*, 313–14 (my emphasis).
79. Quoted in Kelso, *English Gentleman*, 126.
80. See chapter 1.
81. This is not to say that Herbert is unique in emphasizing the experiential component of faith. Christians of every tradition have acknowledged the necessity of coupling holy living with intellectual assent to doctrine. Herbert's uniqueness (as explained earlier in chapter 2) lies in his strong and surprising emphasis on life to the neglect of doctrine. Herbert's focus is squarely ethical (dealing with behavior) while his Puritan colleagues' is more pietistic, intellectual, and supernatural.
82. See chapter 1.

Chapter 4. The Civile Conversation

1. Stefano Guazzo, *The Civile Conversation of M. Steven Guazzo*, trans. George Pettie (1581) and Bartholomew Young (1586), ed. Edward Sullivan, 2 vols. (New York: Alfred A. Knopf, 1925), 1:216. Further quotations from this work in this chapter will be cited in the text by volume and page number.
2. *The Works of George Herbert*, ed. F. E. Hutchinson (Oxford: Clarendon Press, 1941), 224. All quotations from Herbert will be cited in the text by page number and line number from this edition. Used by permission of Oxford University Press.
3. Quoted in John Leon Lievsay, *Stefano Guazzo and the English Renaissance* (Chapel Hill: University of North Carolina Press, 1961), 45.
4. Lievsay, *Guazzo*, 57.
5. Ibid., 53, 48–52.
6. Sullivan in Guazzo, *Civile Conversation,* 1:xli.
7. Lievsay, *Guazzo*, 53.
8. Edward Herbert, *The Autobiography of Edward, Lord Herbert of Cherbury*, ed. Sidney Lee (London: Routledge and Sons, 1886), 42.
9. Hutchinson, *Works of George Herbert*, 570.
10. Ibid., 573.
11. Lievsay believes that Herbert read Guazzo in Italian. He points out: "It is obvious that Herbert was translating and adapting these proverbs, rather than attempting to find English equivalents for them. His free handling of the *sensus,* or theme, rather than the *ipsissima verba,* may account for some of the variations from Guazzian forms" (Lievsay, *Guazzo*, 141).
12. Lievsay, *Guazzo*, 141.
13. Ibid., 142.
14. Ibid., 118–19.
15. Ibid., 143.
16. Ibid., 45.

17. For a discussion of Herbert's familiarity with the Bible, see Chana Bloch, *Spelling the Word: George Herbert and the Bible* (Berkeley: University of California Press, 1985).

18. Neither Hutchinson nor Lievsay have noted these parallel proverbs.

19. Cristina Malcolmson, *George Herbert: A Literary Life* (New York: Palgrave Macmillan, 2004), 149.

20. Ibid.

21. Ronald W. Cooley, *'Full of all knowledg': George Herbert's* Country Parson *and Early Modern Social Discourse* (Toronto: University of Toronto Press, 2004), 102.

22. John Jackson, *Ecclesiastes. The Worthy Church-man* (London: R. More, 1628), 56–57.

23. Ibid., iii.

24. Richard Bernard, *The Faithfull Shepheard: Or the Shepheards Faithfulnesse* (London, 1607), A3.

25. Ibid., 3.

26. Ibid., 5.

27. William Perkins, *Of the Calling of the Ministrie,* 2 parts (London, 1605), 2:17.

28. Ibid., 2:51, 1:21, 1:35.

29. Cooley, *All knowledg*, 12.

30. Perkins, *Of the Calling*, 2:51.

31. Ibid., 2:52.

32. For a fuller discussion see chapter 3 of this study.

33. Guazzo uses the term "conversation" not in the modern sense of talking, but in the now obsolete sense of one's manner of life or behavior, as in the Authorized Version (1611) of the English Bible in 1 Peter 2:12: "Having your conversation honest among the Gentiles that whereas they speak against you as evil doers, they may, by your good works which they shall behold, glorify God in the day of visitation."

34. Cooley, *All knowledg,* 20, 22.

Chapter 5. "Seeming" and "Being"

1. See chapters 1 and 2 of this study.

2. I Samuel 16:7.

3. This is not to say that all courtesy authors believe that seeming is more important than being—although some patently do—but that seeming is the subject of the Renaissance courtesy book.

4. John Leon Lievsay, *Stefano Guazzo and the English Renaissance* (Chapel Hill: University of North Carolina Press, 1961), 45.

5. Ruth Kelso, *The Doctrine of the English Gentleman in the Sixteenth Century* (Gloucester, MA: Peter Smith, 1964), 82. Used by permission of Peter Smith Publishers.

6. Later English courtesy authors, writing out of a more Puritan and middle-class ethos, will transform the courtesy book according to their taste. Rather than "seeming," "doing" often replaces "being" in these works. See

Louis B. Wright, *Middle-Class Culture in Elizabethan England* (Chapel Hill: University of North Carolina Press, 1935), 127. While all courtesy authors prefer to deal with subjects other than "being," our focus is on courtesy books rising out of the older, aristocratic tradition. Herbert's affinity is in fact with these texts and not with the more middle-class manuals beginning to become popular in Herbert's day.

7. Niccolò Machiavelli, *The Prince*, trans. and ed. Robert M. Adams (New York: Norton, 1977), 44–45.

8. Giovanni Della Casa, *Galateo: Of Manners and Behaviours*, ed. Lewis Einstein (Boston: Merrymount Press, 1914), 15–16.

9. Della Casa, *Galateo*, 102.

10. Baldesar Castiglione, *The Book of the Courtier*, Illus., ed. Edgar Mayhew, trans. Charles S. Singleton (New York: Doubleday, 1959), 104. Copyright © 1959 by Charles S. Singleton and Edgar Mayhew. Used by permission of Doubleday, a division of Random House, Inc.

11. Ibid., 136.

12. William Perkins, *Of the Calling of the Ministrie,* 2 parts (London, 1605), 2:19.

13. Castiglione, *Courtier*, 137.

14. See chapter 1 for a fuller discussion of these passages from *The Country Parson.*

15. Machiavelli, *Prince*, 50–51.

16. Castiglione, *Courtier*, 138–39.

17. Ibid., 139.

18. Ibid., 294.

19. Della Casa, *Galateo*, 94.

20. Perkins, *Of the Calling*, 2:16.

21. For a fuller discussion, see chapter 1.

22. See chapter 1 for a more in depth treatment of appearances in "The Parson praying."

23. Castiglione, *Courtier*, 123.

24. Della Casa, *Galateo*, xv.

25. Ibid., 33.

26. Castiglione, *Courtier*, 320.

27. Ibid., 320.

28. Stefano Guazzo, *The Civile Conversation of M. Steven Guazzo,* trans. George Pettie (1581) and Bartholomew Young (1586), ed. Edward Sullivan, 2 vols. (New York: Alfred A. Knopf, 1925), 1:27.

29. Ibid., 1:80–81.

30. Ibid., 1:124.

31. Ibid., 1:125.

32. Ibid, 1:136–37.

33. Ibid., 1:131.

34. Ibid., 1:132.

35. See chapter 3.

36. Guazzo, *Civile Conversation*, 1:126 (my emphasis).

37. I Pet. 2:12.

38. *The Bible, Revised Standard Version* (New York: American Bible Society, 1971).

39. Guazzo, *Civile Conversation*, 1:56.

40. Lievsay explains this difference between Guazzo and Castiglione this way: "Castiglione's idealized figure, though thrown through the accident of his profession into the company of others, is essentially a lone wolf bent upon self-advancement; Guazzo envisages civic man in his total relationships." John Leon Lievsay, *Stefano Guazzo and the English Renaissance* (Chapel Hill: University of North Carolina Press, 1961), 44.

41. Guazzo, *Civile Conversation*, 1:155.

42. Ibid., 2:56.

43. Lievsay, *Guazzo*, 45.

44. Guazzo, *Civile Conversation*, 1:28.

45. Ibid., 1:29.

46. Ibid., 1:30.

47. Ibid., 1:115.

48. Ibid., 1:116.

49. Ibid., 1:160.

50. Ibid., 2:115.

51. See chapters 1 and 2.

52. Guazzo, *Civile Conversation*, 1:28–29.

53. Ibid., 1:115.

54. Ibid., 1:116.

55. The Puritans tended to stress the individual's experience of salvation and sanctification. Here Herbert, on the other hand, is in keeping with the High Church tendency to view the spiritual life and even salvation in corporate terms—in terms of the "whole church."

56. Lievsay, *Guazzo*, 45.

57. Guazzo, *Civile Conversation*, 1:148.

58. Ibid., 1:155.

59. Ibid., 1:153.

60. Ibid., 1:107.

61. Ibid., 1:160–61.

62. Ibid., 1:111. Here the difference between Guazzo and a Puritan like Perkins (who would rather have his minister humble than seek praise for himself) is clear.

63. Ibid., 1:115–16.

64. Ibid., 1:163.

65. Ibid., 1:213.

66. See chapters 1 and 2 and the first half of this chapter.

67. Guazzo, *Civile Conversation*, 1:159.

68. Ibid., 1:142.

69. Herbert's concern for the church building is documented through records from the time. Amy Charles tells us that in 1630 Herbert and his new wife were "beggarly" because he had spent two hundred pounds on repairing the church and rectory. Amy Charles, *A Life of George Herbert* (Ithaca, NY: Cornell University Press, 1977), 154.

70. See chapter 2 for a fuller discussion on this topic.

71. Appearances (especially those of the pastor and church) are open for public scrutiny and held in common among members of a parish. Because—in keeping with the High Church tendency—the spiritual life assumes a strongly communal and societal form for Herbert, outer forms can indeed contribute to the edification of one's neighbor.

72. Article Twenty of the *Thirty-nine Articles* is frequently glossed with these two verses. But the gloss is used to defend Anglican ceremonies, not the actual appearances of church buildings. See for example Burnet's or Beveridge's expositions of the Articles. And while he is not alone in such proof texting, Herbert must take these verses entirely out of context to make his point. I Cor. 14 has nothing at all to do with walls, floors, pulpit, or communion table. Paul is writing instead on guidelines for glossolalia (speaking in tongues) in the church.

73. See chapter 1.

Conclusion

1. Stefano Guazzo, *The Civile Conversation of M. Steven Guazzo,* trans. George Pettie (1581) and Bartholomew Young (1586), ed. Edward Sullivan, 2 vols. (New York: Alfred A. Knopf, 1925), 1:213.

2. Even such "externall and indifferent things . . . put them to great shame who deny the Scripture to be perfect."–*The Works of George Herbert*, ed. F. E. Hutchinson (Oxford: Clarendon Press, 1941), 246:33. Used by permission of Oxford University Press.

3. The skeptic is persuaded by considering that "God cannot be wanting to them in Doctrine, to whom he is so gracious in life." (Hutchinson, *Works of George Herbert*, 263:19–21).

4. Tuve and Martz, along with Stanley Stewart and others, trace Herbert's heritage largely to medieval and Roman Catholic origins, Summers and Lewalski to Reformation and Protestant ones. Richard Strier, William Halewood, and Chana Bloch followed Lewalski's lead and elucidate the peculiarly Protestant and biblical influences on Herbert's poetry. Other critics have followed on in this subdebate, culminating in what G. E. Veith, Jr. called "The Religious Wars in George Herbert Criticism."

5. Rosemond Tuve, *A Reading of George Herbert* (London: Faber and Faber, 1952), 136.

6. Arnold Stein, *George Herbert's Lyrics* (Baltimore: Johns Hopkins University Press, 1968), 83.

7. Ibid., 139.

8. Ibid., 143.

9. Ibid., 202.

10. Stanley Fish, *The Living Temple: George Herbert and Catechizing* (Berkeley: University of California Press, 1978), 26.

11. This question is less pressing in relation to the poems in which the first person narrator is absent, but it is particularly relevant when we consider Herbert's "discovery" poems, poems in the course of which the narrator changes or

learns something. (Chana Bloch identifies "Redemption," "The Thanksgiving," "Jordon, II," "The Holdfast," "Affliction, I," "The Crosse," and "The Collar" as poems of discovery.—Chana Bloch, *Spelling the Word: George Herbert and the Bible* (Berkley: University of California Press, 1985), 148.

12. In broad terms the concept of literary form shaping spiritual experience is not new to Herbert criticism. Louis Martz explored the relationship between Herbert's religious life and meditative manuals. Lewalski, Strier, and Bloch show the influences of Protestant treatises and the Bible on Herbert's thinking. Given these (and other) influences the critical issue still remains. While attentiveness to religious forms may have shaped Herbert's spiritual biography, we still need a way to understand how Herbert's spiritual biography is related to his poetry. I suggest that we consider Herbert's poetry as in some way catalyzing and influencing his religious experiences.

Bibliography

Adolph, Robert. *The Rise of Modern Prose Style*. Cambridge: MIT Press, 1968.

Ainger, Alfred "George Herbert." *English Prose* 2 (1894): 202–04.

Allen, Don Cameron. "Style and Certitude." *Journal of English Literary History* 15 (1948): 167–75.

Ames, William. *The Marrow of Theology*. 1629. Edited by John D. Eusden. Boston: Pilgrim Press, 1968.

Ascham, Roger. *The Schoolmaster*. Edited by Lawrence V. Ryan. Ithaca, NY: Cornell University Press, 1967.

The Authorized Version of the English Bible. 1611. Edited by William Aldis Wright. Cambridge: Cambridge University Press, 1909.

Richard Baxter, *Preface to Poetical Fragments* (London, 1681), quoted in Hutchinson, *Works of George Herbert,* xliv. Used by permission of Oxford University Press.

———. *The Practical Works of Richard Baxter*. London, 1707.

———. *The Reformed Pastor*. 1656. New York: The American Tract Society, 1829.

Bell, Ilona. "Setting Foot into Divinity: George Herbert and the English Reformation." *Modern Language Quarterly* 38 (1977): 219–41.

Bernard, Richard. *The Faithfull Shepheard: Or the Shepheards Faithfulnesse*. London. 1607.

Beveridge, William. *Ecclesia Anglicana Ecclesia Catholica OR The Doctrine of the Church of England Consonant To Scripture, Reason, and Fathers: in a Discourse upon the Thirty Nine Articles Agreed Upon in the Convocation Held At London 1562*. Oxford: Oxford University Press, 1847.

Blau, Sheridan D. "The Poet as Casuist: Herbert's 'Church Porch.'" *Genre* 4 (1971): 142–52.

Bloch, Chana. *Spelling the Word: George Herbert and the Bible*. Berkeley: University of California Press, 1985.

The Book of Common Prayer. 1559. Edited by John E. Booty. Washington: Folger Books, 1976.

The Book of Common Prayer. 1604. London: Wm Pickering, 1844.

Bottrall, Margaret. *George Herbert*. London: Wyman and Sons, 1954.

———. "George Herbert and 'The Country Parson'." *The Listener* (April 3, 1952): 558–59.

Brathwaite, Richard. *The English Gentleman.* 1630. London: John Dawson, 1641.

Breton, Nicholas. "The Goode and the Badde." In *The Works in Verse and Prose of Nicholas Breton.* 1616. Edited by Alexander B. Gorsart. New York: AMS Press, 1966.

Burnet, Gilbert. *A Discourse of the Pastoral Care.* 1692. London: Rivingtons and Cochran, 1821.

———. *An Exposition of the Thirty-Nine Articles of the Church of England.* 1699. London: R. Roberts at the Rose and Crown, 1700.

Bush, Douglas. *English Literature in the Earlier Seventeenth Century, 1600–1660.* London: Oxford University Press, 1962.

Calvin, John. *Calvin's New Testament Commentaries.* Edited by David W. Torrance and Thomas F. Torrance. 12 Vols. Grand Rapids, MI: Eerdmans, 1964.

Castiglione, Baldesar. *The Book of the Courtier.* Translated by Charles S. Singleton. New York: Doubleday, 1959.

Charles, Amy M. *A Life of George Herbert.* Ithaca, NY: Cornell University Press, 1977.

Clarke, Elizabeth. "The Character of a Non-Laudian Country Parson." *The Review of English Studies,* New Series 54, no. 216 (2003): 478–96.

Cleland, James. *The Institution of a Young Nobleman.* 1607. New York: Scholars' Facsimiles & Reprints, 1948.

Cooley, Ronald W. *'Full of all knowledg': George Herbert's* Country Parson *and Early Modern Social Discourse.* Toronto: University of Toronto Press, 2003.

Craik, Henry. *English Prose.* Vol. 2. New York: Macmillan, 1894.

Cremeans, Charles Davis. *The Reception of Calvinistic Thought in England.* Urbana: University of Illinois Press, 1949.

Croll, Morris. *Style, Rhetoric, and Rhythm: Essays by Morris W. Croll.* Edited by J. Max Patrick et al. Princeton, NJ: Princeton University Press, 1966.

Della Casa, Giovanni. *Galateo: Of Manners and Behaviours.* Edited by Lewis Einstein. Boston: Merrymount Press, 1914.

Di Cesare, Mario and Mignani, Rigo. *A Concordance to the Complete Writings of George Herbert.* Ithaca, NY: Cornell University Press, 1977.

Doerksen, Daniel W. "'Too Good for Those Times': Politics and the Publication of George Herbert's *The Country Parson," Seventeenth-Century News* 49 (Spring–Summer 1991): 10–13.

———. *Conforming to the Word: Herbert, Donne, and the English Church before Laud.* Lewisburg, PA: Bucknell University Press, 1997.

Earle, John. *Microcosmography.* 1628. Edited by Philip Bliss. London: White and Cochrane, 1811.

Ellis, Clement. *The Gentile Sinner.* 1664. Oxford: Henry Hall, 1679.

Elyot, Thomas. *The Book Named the Governor.* 1531. Edited by S. E. Lehmberg. London: Dent, 1962.

Endicott, Annabel M. "'The Soul in Paraphrase': George Herbert's 'Library.'" *Renaissance News* 19 (1966): 14–16.

Fisch, Harold. "The Puritans and the Reform of Prose Style." *A Journal of English Literary History* 19 (1952): 229–48.

Fish, Stanley. *The Living Temple: George Herbert and Catechizing.* Berkeley: University of California Press, 1978.

———. *Self-Consuming Artifacts: The Experience of Seventeenth-Century Literature.* Berkeley: University of California Press, 1972.

———. ed. *Seventeenth Century Prose: Modern Essays in Criticism.* New York: Oxford University Press, 1971.

Florio, John. *Second Frutes.* 1591. Edited by R. C. Simonini. Gainesville, FL: Scholars' Facsimiles & Reprints, 1953.

Fuller, Thomas. *The Holy State, and The Profane State.* 1642. Edited by James Nichols. London: Thomas Tegg, 1841.

Gallagher, Michael P. "Rhetoric, Style, and George Herbert." *Journal of English Literary History* 37 (1970): 495–516.

Gardiner, James. *Advice to the Clergy of the Diocese of Lincoln.* London: The Star in Ludgate-Street, 1697.

The Geneva Bible. 1560. Madison: University of Wisconsin Press, 1969.

George, Charles H. and Katherine. *The Protestant Mind of the English Reformation, 1570–1640.* Princeton, NJ: Princeton University Press, 1961.

Greenblatt, Stephen. *Renaissance Self Fashioning.* Chicago: University of Chicago Press, 1980.

Guazzo, Stefano. *The Civile Conversation of M. Steven Guazzo.* Translated by George Pettie (1581) and Bartholomew Young (1586). Edited by Edward Sullivan. 2 vols. New York: Alfred A. Knopf, 1925.

Halewood, William H. *The Poetry of Grace: Reformation Themes and Structures in English Seventeenth-Century Poetry.* New Haven, CT: Yale University Press, 1970.

Hall, David D. *The Faithful Shepherd: A History of the New England Ministry in the Seventeenth Century.* Chapel Hill: University of North Carolina Press, 1972.

Haller, William. *The Rise of Puritanism.* New York: Columbia University Press, 1938.

Hamilton, K. G. *The Two Harmonies: Prose and Poetry in the Seventeenth Century.* Oxford: Clarendon Press, 1963.

Hart, Tindal A. *Clergy and Society, 1600–1800.* London: SPCK, 1968.

———. *The Country Clergy in Elizabethan and Stuart Times, 1558–1660.* London: Phoenix House, 1958.

Hazlitt, W. C. (No title; article denying Herbert's authorship of *Outlandish Proverbs.*) *Collections and Notes.* 1867–76, 1876.

Herbert, Edward. *The Autobiography of Edward, Lord Herbert of Cherbury.* Edited by Sidney Lee. London: George Routledge & Sons, 1886.

Herbert, George. *The Works of George Herbert.* Edited by F. E. Hutchinson. Oxford: Clarendon Press, 1941.

———. *George Herbert's Country Parson.* Edited by H. C. Beeching. Oxford: Oxford University Press, 1898.

———. *The English Poems of George Herbert.* Edited by C. A. Patrides. London: Dent, 1974.

Hinman, Robert B. "The 'Verser' at the Temple Door: Herbert's 'The Church-Porch.'" In *Too Rich to Clothe the Sunne: Essays on George Herbert,* Edited by Claude J. Summers and Ted-Larry Pebworth, 55–75. Pittsburgh, PA: University of Pittsburgh Press, 1980.

Hirst, Derek, and Strier, Richard. *Writing and Political Engagement in Seventeenth-Century England.* Cambridge: Cambridge University Press, 1999.

Hodgkins, Christopher. *Authority, Church and Society in George Herbert: Return to the Middle Way.* Columbia: University of Missouri Press, 1993.

———. " ' Showing Holy': Herbert and the Rhetoric of Sanctity." In *New Perspectives on the Seventeenth-Century English Religious Lyric,* edited by John R. Roberts, 222–36. Columbia, MO: University of Missouri Press, 1994.

Jackson, John. *Ecclesiastes. The Worthy Church-man.* London: R. More, 1628.

Javitch, Daniel. *Poetry and Courtliness in Renaissance England.* Princeton, NJ: Princeton University Press, 1978.

Jones, Richard Foster. *The Seventeenth Century.* Stanford, CA: Stanford University Press, 1951.

Jordon, Wilbur K. *The Development of Religious Toleration in England from the Accession of James I to the Convention of the Long Parliament, 1603–1640.* Cambridge, MA: Harvard University Press, 1936.

Kelso, Ruth. *The Doctrine of the English Gentleman in the Sixteenth Century.* Gloucester, MA: Peter Smith, 1964.

Kessner, Carole. "Entering 'The Church-Porch': Herbert and Wisdom Poetry." *George Herbert Journal* 4 (1971): 142–52.

Kneidel, Gregory. "Herbert and Exactness." *English Literary Renaissance* 36, issue 2 (2006): 173–303.

Kollmeier, Harold Henry. "'A Mark to Aim At' Genre and Sensibility in George Herbert's *Country Parson.*" PhD diss., State University of New York, Abstract in *Dissertation Abstracts International* 37 (1976): 1566A.

———. "The Country Parson in its Time." In *Like Season'd Timber: New Essays on George Herbert.* Edited by Edmund Miller and Robert DiYanni. New York: Peter Lang, 1987.

Krapp, George. *The Rise of English Literary Prose.* New York: Ungar, 1947.

Lee, Patricia A. "The Ideal of the English Gentleman in the Early Seventeenth Century." PhD diss., Columbia, Abstract in *Dissertation Abstracts International* 28 (1967): 635A.

Lewalski, Barbara Kiefer. *Protestant Poetics and the Seventeenth-Century Religious Lyric.* Princeton, NJ: Princeton University Press, 1968.

Lievsay, John Leon. *Stefano Guazzo and the English Renaissance.* Chapel Hill: University of North Carolina Press, 1961.

Luther, Martin. *Luther's Works.* Edited by Hilton C. Oswand and Jaroslav Pelikan. 30 Vols. St. Louis, MO: Concordia Publishing House, 1972.

Machiavelli, Niccolò. *The Prince.* Translated and edited by Robert M. Adams. New York: Norton, 1977.

Mahood, M. M. *Poetry and Humanism.* New York: Norton, 1949.

Malcolmson, Cristina. *George Herbert: A Literary Life.* New York: Palgrave Macmillan, 2004.

———. "George Herbert's *Country Parson* and the Character of Social Identity." *Studies in Philology* 85, no. 2 (Spring 1988): 245–66.

Marcus, Leah Sinanoglou. "George Herbert and the Anglican Plain Style." In *Too Rich to Clothe the Sunne: Essays on George Herbert.* Edited by Claude J. Summers and Ted-Larry Pebworth, 179–93. Pittsburgh, PA: University of Pittsburgh Press, 1980.

Martz, Louis. *The Poetry of Meditation: A Study in English Religious History of the Seventeenth Century.* New Haven, CT: Yale University Press, 1962.

Mason, John E. *Gentlefolk in the Making: Studies in the History of English Courtesy Literature and Related Topics from 1531–1774.* Philadelphia: University of Pennsylvania Press, 1935.

Mather, Cotton. *Manaductio Ad Ministerium: Directions for a Candidate of the Ministry.* 1726. New York: AMS Press, 1938.

Mayor, J. E. B. "Herbert's *Jocula Prudentum*: Ferrar's Life." *Notes and Queries,* 2nd ser., 3 (Feb 14, 1857): 130–31.

McGee, J. Sears. *The Godly Man in Stuart England: Anglicans, Puritans, and the Two Tables, 1620–1670.* New Haven, CT: Yale University Press, 1976.

Miller, Perry. *The New England Mind: The Seventeenth Century.* New York: MacMillan, 1939.

Mitchell, W. Fraser. *English Pulpit Oratory from Andrewes to Tillotson.* New York: Russell & Russell, 1962.

Mulcaster, Richard. *Mulcaster's Elementarie.* 1582. Edited by E. T. Campagnac. Oxford: Clarendon Press, 1925.

Nicolson, Harold. *Good Behaviour: Being a Study of Certain Types of Civility.* New York: Doubleday, 1956.

Noyes, Gertrude E. *Bibliography of Courtesy and Conduct Books in Seventeenth-Century England.* New Haven, CT: Tuttle, Morehouse & Taylor, 1937.

Overbury, Sir Thomas. *A Wife . . . of Sir T. Overburye . . . many witty characters.* 1614. London: John Playfere, 1664.

Parallel New Testament in Greek and English. Grand Rapids, MI: Zondervan Bible Publishers, 1975.

Peacham, Henry. *Compleat Gentleman.* 1634. Oxford: Clarendon Press, 1906.

Perkins, William. *Of the Calling of the Ministrie.* 2 parts. London, 1605.

———. *The works of that famous and worthy minister in Christ in the Vniversitie of Cambridge, M. William Perkins, Newly corrected according to his owne copies.* London: John Legatt, 1631.

Revised Standard Version of the Bible. 2nd ed. London: Oxford University Press, 1971.

Richardson, Caroline Francis. *English Preachers and Preaching, 1640–1670.* London: Society for Promoting Christian Knowledge, 1928.

Rickey, Mary Ellen. *Utmost Art: Complexity in the Verse of George Herbert.* Lexington: University of Kentucky Press, 1966.

Roberts, John R. ed. *New Perspectives on the Seventeenth-Century Religious Lyric.* Columbia, MO: University of Missouri Press, 1994.

Ross, M. M. "George Herbert and the Humanist Tradition." *University of Toronto Quarterly* 16, no. 2 (1947): 160–182.

Schoenfeldt, Michael C. *Prayer and Power: George Herbert and Renaissance Courtship.* Chicago: University of Chicago Press, 1991.

Singleton, Marion White. *God's Courtier: Configuring a Different Grace in George Herbert's Temple.* New York: Cambridge University Press, 1987.

Stein, Arnold. *George Herbert's Lyrics.* Baltimore, MD: Johns Hopkins University Press, 1968.

Stewart, Stanley, *George Herbert.* Boston: Twayne Publishers, 1986.

Stone, Lawrence. *The Crisis of the Aristocracy: 1558–1641.* Oxford: Clarendon Press, 1965.

Strier, Richard. *Love Known: Theology and Experience in George Herbert's Poetry.* Chicago: University of Chicago Press, 1983.

Sullivan, Sir Edward, *Introduction to The Civile Conversation by Stefano Guazzo,* v–xcii. New York: Alfred A. Knopf, 1925.

Summers, Joseph H. *George Herbert: His Religion and Art.* Cambridge, MA: Harvard University Press, 1954.

Swartz, Douglas J. "Discourse and Direction: *A Priest to the Temple, or, the Country Parson* and the Elaboration of Sovereign Rule." *Criticism* 36, no. 2 (Spring 1994): 189–212.

Taylor, Jeremy. "Clerus Domini or Rules and Advices to the Clergy of the Dioceses of Down and Conner," In *The Curate of Souls.* 1661. Edited by John R. H. Moorman. London: SPCK, 1958, 1–26.

———. *The Rule and Exercises of Holy Dying.* 1819. New York: Arno Press, 1977.

Thompson, Elbert N. S. *Literary Bypaths of the Renaissance.* New Haven, CT: Yale University Press, 1924.

Traill, Robert. *The Works of Robert Traill: Vols. 1 and 2.* 1810. Edinburgh: The Banner of Truth Trust, 1975.

Tuve, Rosemond. *A Reading of George Herbert.* London: Faber and Faber, 1952.

Veith, Gene E. *Reformation Spirituality: The Religion of George Herbert.* Lewisburg, PA: Bucknell University Press, 1985.

———. "The Religious Wars in George Herbert Criticism: Reinterpreting Seventeenth-Century Anglicanism." *George Herbert Journal* 11, no. 2 (Spring 1988): 19–35.

Vendler, Helen. *The Poetry of George Herbert.* Cambridge, MA: Harvard University Press, 1975.

Wall, John N. *Transformations of the Word: Spenser, Herbert and Vaughn.* Athens, GA: University of Georgia Press, 1998.

Walton, Izaak. *The Life of Mr. George Herbert.* London: R. Marriott, 1670.

Watson, Thomas. *A Body of Practical Divinity.* London: Bible & Three Crowns, 1686.

———. *The Ten Commandments.* 1692. London: The Banner of Truth Trust, 1970.

Webber, Joan. "Stylistics: A Bridging of Life and Art in Seventeenth Century Studies." *New Literary History* 2 (1970–71): 283–96.

———. *The Eloquent "I": Style and Self in Seventeenth Century Prose.* Madison, WI: University of Wisconsin Press, 1968.

White, Helen C. *English Devotional Literature [Prose], 1600–1640.* New York: Haskell House, 1966.

———. *The Tudor Books of Private Devotion.* Madison: University of Wisconsin Press, 1951.

Williamson, George. *The Senecan Amble.* Chicago: University of Chicago Press, 1951.

Wilson, F. P. *Seventeenth Century Prose.* Berkeley: University of California Press, 1960.

Wolberg, Kristine. "All Possible Art: George Herbert's *The Country Parson* and Courtesy." *John Donne Journal* 8, nos. 1 & 2 (1989): 167–89.

———. "George Herbert's *The Country Parson* and Stefano Guazzo's *The Civile Conversation.*" *George Herbert Journal* 27, nos. 1 &2 (Fall 2003/Spring 2004): 105–18.

Wright, H. G. "Was George Herbert the Author of *Jacula Prudentum?" Review of English Studies* 11 (April 1935): 139–44.

Wright, Louis B. *Middle-Class Culture in Elizabethan England.* Chapel Hill: University of North Carolina Press, 1935.

Yeowell, James. "Was George Herbert the Compiler of *Jacula Prudentum or Outlandish Proverbs* etc.?" *Notes and Queries,* 2nd ser., 3 (1857): 88–89.

Index